# CRYPTOCURRENCY INVESTING

DISCOVER THE MOST LUCRATIVE WAYS TO PROFIT WITH CRYPTO, BITCOIN, ETHEREUM, ALTCOINS, NFTS, AND BLOCKCHAIN—MASTER THE ART OF WEALTH WITHOUT LIMITS

LUCAS STERLING

TOP TIER PRESS

Published under the author brand **Lucas Sterling**



**Disclaimer Notice**

The information in this publication is provided for educational and informational purposes only. While every effort has been made to ensure accuracy, no warranties of any kind are expressed or implied. The publisher and author make no representations regarding completeness or suitability of the material contained herein.

Readers acknowledge that neither the author nor the publisher is engaged in rendering medical, legal, financial, or professional advice. The content is based on sources believed to be reliable, but readers should consult qualified professionals before applying any techniques or practices mentioned.

By reading this work, the reader agrees that under no circumstances shall the author or publisher be liable for any loss or damages—direct or indirect—resulting from the use of the information contained within this book.

# CONTENTS

# INTRODUCTION

Imagine waking up one morning and discovering that the financial world has fundamentally changed, with new rules, new players, and entirely new ways to create wealth. In many ways, that is precisely what is happening right now. We are experiencing a digital financial revolution in which cryptocurrencies and blockchain technology are transforming not only our understanding of money but also the ability for anyone, anywhere, to build genuine wealth from the ground up.

If you are holding this book, chances are you have already felt the tremors of this shift. Maybe it was a friend who suddenly started talking about Bitcoin at dinner, or a news story highlighting astonishing gains and equally shocking losses. Perhaps you have even experimented with cryptocurrency, buying a few coins through an app and watching the prices rise and fall. Whether you are simply curious or cautiously optimistic, there is a good reason why you, and millions of others, are asking: Can I actually profit from crypto? And if so, what is the smartest way to do it?

Let us be clear. Crypto is no longer just a buzzword for tech enthusiasts or a playground for risk-takers. It is becoming the new frontier of modern wealth building, one filled with both opportunity and risk, much like the gold rush or the early days of Wall Street. Yet for every genuine chance to succeed in this space, there is also hype, misinformation, and the occasional scam. The headlines often make it seem as though everyone is either getting rich overnight or losing everything they own. The truth lies somewhere in between, and it rewards those who approach this world with clear eyes and a thoughtful plan.

This book exists to show that navigating the crypto landscape does not have to be confusing, overly technical, or limited to insiders. It is written for ambitious people who want to learn, not just watch from the sidelines, as this new asset class evolves. You might be a professional looking to diversify beyond stocks and real estate, a freelancer aiming to grow your savings, or an entrepreneur seeking financial freedom on your own terms. Maybe you follow finance channels, read newsletters, or listen to podcasts in search of your next opportunity. What unites readers like you is a willingness to take action, a tolerance for calculated risk, and a desire to understand the forces shaping our financial future rather than simply chasing them.

The first myth I want to dispel is the belief that crypto is a passing fad, destined for oblivion like dot-com penny stocks or Beanie Babies. In reality, the technology behind cryptocurrencies, known as blockchain, has already rewritten the rules of ownership, trust, and value exchange around the world. More importantly, the growth of crypto assets is being driven not by speculation alone but by genuine innovation. Entire sectors of the economy are being reimagined. From decentralized finance (DeFi) protocols that eliminate middlemen, to non-fungible tokens (NFTs) that open new markets in art and entertainment, to stablecoins that challenge the dominance of national currencies, crypto is reshaping the financial landscape in real time.

At the same time, it is important to be honest. Alongside extraordinary stories of everyday people earning life-changing profits, there are also accounts of devastating losses. The volatility can be intimidating, the jargon confusing, and the sheer number of options overwhelming. There is a steep learning curve, yet it remains one of the most dynamic and potentially rewarding areas to explore as an investor today. The difference between those who succeed and those who struggle is not insider information or advanced technical knowledge. It comes down to having a clear, actionable plan and the willingness to learn, adapt, and make informed decisions.

That is exactly what this book aims to deliver. In the chapters ahead, you will move beyond the noise and the memes to gain a solid understanding of how crypto works, why it matters, and, most importantly, how to participate wisely in this evolving market. You will discover what makes assets such as Bitcoin, Ethereum, and other altcoins unique, and learn how to evaluate which projects are worth your attention and investment. We will explore multiple approaches for generating income, from simple buy-and-hold strategies to trading techniques and emerging opportunities in staking, DeFi, and NFTs. Each method carries its own risks and rewards. By the end, you will have the knowledge and confidence to build a portfolio tailored to your goals, whether you seek short-term gains or long-term generational wealth.

Crypto investing is not about chasing moonshots or falling for hype. It is about stacking small, smart decisions that add up over time. If you are reading this, you are likely not afraid of a little risk, but you are also wise enough to demand clarity before making a move. That is why I promise no fluff, no empty claims, and no vague advice. You will find only strategies and insights that help you profit from crypto, explained in plain language, supported by real examples, and grounded in realistic expectations. Every chapter is designed to give you practical steps you can apply immediately, whether you have one hundred or one hundred thousand dollars to invest.

We will start simple and build from there, making sure each concept makes sense before moving forward. You do not need to be a programmer, a math expert, or a full-time trader. All you need is curiosity, ambition, and the willingness to learn. Together we will break down complex topics into clear, manageable lessons using relatable examples and straightforward guidance. When technical terms appear, you will find explanations that go beyond definitions, giving you context so you understand why something matters and how it affects your results.

It is worth emphasizing that the stakes are real, and so are the opportunities. As banks, governments, and corporations race to adapt to rapid technological change, early adopters who educate themselves and act strategically have a rare chance to get ahead. However, crypto is not a get-rich-quick scheme, and luck alone rarely leads to lasting success. If you are hoping for a hidden shortcut, this is not that kind of book. What you will gain instead is a solid foundation, built on the same mindset and tools used by successful investors who endure both bull and bear markets, capitalize on trends, and steadily grow wealth across different cycles.

By the end of this journey, you will know how to analyze coins, recognize potential scams, and evaluate projects based on real value rather than hype. You will understand how to use wallets and exchanges safely, manage risk with confidence, and create a personalized investment plan that matches your timeline and risk tolerance. Whether your goal is to supplement your income, save for the future, or achieve financial independence from traditional systems, you will finish this book ready to make smarter, more confident choices in the fast-changing world of crypto.

The digital frontier of wealth is wide open, and the barriers to entry have never been lower. The only true limit is your willingness to learn and take action. If you are ready to move beyond fear and confusion, to cut through the noise, and to see how ordinary people are using crypto to build extraordinary opportunities, then this book is for you. Let us step forward into the future of finance together, with clarity and purpose.

# UNLOCK YOUR CRYPTO MASTERY TOOLKIT

*Ready to take control of your digital wealth with clarity and confidence?*

As a thank-you for reading this book, I've created a practical guide: **The Crypto Mastery Toolkit.** This hands-on guide simplifies key crypto concepts, helps you secure your assets, and builds confidence as you manage your digital wealth. It's designed to help you learn and apply crypto knowledge with ease and clarity.

*What's included in this resource:*

- Understand key crypto concepts and terminology
- Learn strategies for secure asset management
- Discover best practices for wallets, exchanges, and safety
- Develop confidence navigating today's digital economy

**Access Your Companion Workbook**

Visit: **https://content.toptierpress.com/unlock-free-crypto-mastery-toolkit**

Or scan the QR code below to get instant access!

# CHAPTER 1
# CRYPTO 101 – WHAT IT IS AND WHY IT MATTERS

What if everything you thought you knew about money was already outdated? What if the systems we have trusted for decades, including banks, governments, and financial institutions, were no longer the only way to manage, move, or grow your wealth? Imagine a world where you can send funds anywhere in minutes, without needing anyone's permission or interference. This is not a distant vision of the future. It is happening right now, and it is transforming how people across the globe think about money, power, and access.

For many, cryptocurrency still feels like a puzzle filled with technical terms and confusing hype. Yet beneath all that noise lies a simple, powerful idea that can redefine financial freedom and opportunity. The shift from traditional finance to digital currencies challenges long-standing rules and opens the door to new ways of investing, saving, and taking control of your financial life. Whether you are curious, cautious, or ready to dive in, understanding this change is the first step toward making smart and confident choices about your future.

## Comparing Cryptocurrency with Traditional Finance and Foundational Concepts

The traditional financial world centers around trusted middlemen banks, governments, stock exchanges who manage the flow of money, approve transactions, and make the rules. When someone deposits their salary in a bank, the bank holds those funds, tracks their account, and verifies their money is legitimate. If they want to send money overseas, a network of banks, payment processors, and sometimes governments get involved. These layers mean international transfers can take days, come with heavy fees, and be subject to approval or delays. Account access remains at the bank's discretion, with the possibility of restrictions, freezes, or reversals if the institution suspects trouble.

Cryptocurrency rewrites these rules. Digital coins like Bitcoin and Ethereum use technology to offer direct control over funds, sidestepping the need for central managers. With crypto, sending value to someone anywhere in the world happens on a shared digital network without bank approval. Transactions can settle in minutes even across continents, often for much lower fees, regardless of local banking hours or government borders. The keys to your crypto wallet put control back in your hands, instead of letting a distant institution decide what you can or cannot do with your money.

Traditional finance stores value in physical banks or records in electronic ledgers managed by each institution. Payments and investments route through trusted third parties that can introduce cost, delay, and risk. Crypto value, in contrast, lives on a shared public blockchain. No single entity owns or controls this ledger; every participant can see and verify transactions for themselves.

This structure not only changes how people move and store money but also who gets to participate. Opening a crypto wallet requires no paperwork or approval; anyone with an internet connection can use it.

## *Core Principles Shaping Crypto*

### Decentralization

The most important shift crypto offers is decentralization. Power, once consolidated in banks or central authorities, is distributed over countless computers known as nodes. Each node keeps a copy of the blockchain and validates new transactions independently. Unlike a bank, which can shut down access if a branch experiences an outage, a decentralized network stays running even if parts of it go offline. In the case of Bitcoin, people around the world maintain the same transaction database, so the service doesn't depend on a single organization or location.

### Transparency

Blockchains act as public ledgers, digital books open for anyone to inspect. Every transaction ever made on a network like Ethereum or Bitcoin is visible to all users. If someone wants to check where their funds have moved or confirm the legitimacy of an address, the public record is available at any time. This transparency gives crypto a built-in self-audit feature. It fosters trust, reduces the room for manipulation, and discourages shady behavior. In traditional finance, auditing account histories can require costly legal action or negotiation with banks that may refuse to share data. In crypto, users are empowered to inspect and verify anything they want freely.

### Financial Sovereignty

Crypto hands over the reins to the individual, offering full control over assets. Only the owner of private keys can move the coins in their digital wallet; no manager, clerk, or intermediary can interfere. Consider an example: someone living in one country who wants to send money home to parents abroad. Using a bank wire, the process may involve multiple checks, approvals, and steep international fees. With crypto, sending funds means authorizing a transaction from wallet to wallet. The money arrives in minutes, and no third party can freeze or block it. This level of access isn't possible with regular checking accounts, which are vulnerable to institutional controls.

## *How Blockchain Transforms the Economy*

At the core of every cryptocurrency is blockchain technology. Imagine a digital notebook shared with everyone, where each page contains a group of transactions. Once a page is filled, it is locked in and linked forever to the next, creating a chain. Anyone can flip through these pages and review transaction details, ensuring nothing gets altered or erased. This design makes fraud very hard and guarantees a full history of what happened and when.

Blockchains let people trade, lend, and store value directly. Peer-to-peer transactions cut out middlemen such as payment processors or notaries, making deals quicker and cheaper. Businesses have started to use blockchain to track goods through supply chains knowing if a bottle of olive oil really comes from Italy, for example, or if a diamond was sourced ethically. Companies can prove the origin and journey of their products to consumers using blockchain entries.

In finance, decentralized applications replace what banks once did. People can borrow, lend, earn interest, or insure assets through code-based contracts open for anyone to see and use. Some use blockchains for digital collectibles and art known as NFTs which provide ownership records that can't be copied or faked. The impact stretches beyond banking, shaking up every line of business that used to depend on trusted third parties.

These changes open doors. Individuals can join global markets, invest, and own assets without seeking approval from big institutions. Each of these features unlocks new opportunities for people to manage, grow, and protect their wealth in ways once reserved for industry insiders. As readers take in these distinctions and principles, it becomes clear how the world of crypto invites a fresh, more direct approach to building financial independence and exploring the future of investing.

## Crypto's Disruptive Nature and Personal Relevance

Decentralization stands at the heart of the disruption caused by cryptocurrency in the world of finance. In traditional systems, transactions must be approved by banks or credit unions, which act as powerful middlemen. Imagine needing a banker's sign-off just to send money to a friend in another country, then waiting several days with fees deducted at every step. With crypto, individuals send value directly to anyone on the globe almost instantly, with no approval or bank gatekeeping required. This feature alone introduces a new sense of freedom, like being able to write and mail your letter anywhere in the world without relying on a postal worker to read or stamp it first. The blockchain, a digital ledger that records every transaction publicly, replaces centralized oversight with transparency everyone can trust.

In this way, cryptocurrencies like Bitcoin or Ethereum challenge long-standing structures by removing gatekeepers and giving power back to users. The rules of the network are enforced by software, not by humans behind a counter. The implications reach further than faster payments; they allow people who have never had access to formal banking to transact, save, and invest with just an internet connection. Crypto does not care about citizenship, employment history, or the status of your local economy. If you have a smartphone or computer, you can set up a free wallet, buy or receive tiny amounts of any coin, and become a participant.

Traditional investing often comes with barriers: high minimum deposits, lengthy approval processes, and requirements to pass credit or identification checks. Crypto's entry points are much easier to access. You do not need to "qualify" to open a wallet, nor do you need permission to participate in a decentralized finance (DeFi) protocol. With DeFi tools, regular people access peer-to-peer lending, borrowing, and earning interest by supplying funds directly into liquidity pools. Many services let users buy fractions of coins, making it possible to start with even a few dollars. There are platforms where you can stake coins to support the network and earn rewards, or pool your money with others to maximize returns. These opportunities appear instantly on your screen, without negotiation with a broker or bank manager.

Accessibility does not stop at low entry thresholds. The cryptocurrency market operates continuously, with prices fluctuating and traders engaging in transactions around the clock, every day of the year. There are no "market closed" notices or downtime for holidays. This setup fits those who want to invest or manage assets on their own schedule, or those across time zones who can't always work within the restrictions of traditional trading hours. Crypto treats users equally, whether they come from a major economic hub or a small, remote village.

Several practical reasons make crypto worth a spot in an investor's future plans. One, crypto gives a real way to diversify your portfolio. Its price moves are often uncorrelated with the swings in stocks or bonds. For instance, during some global downturns, while traditional markets faltered, Bitcoin not only held value but sometimes climbed. By including crypto, an investor may reduce overall risk and build a portfolio that can weather situations where other assets struggle.

Another draw lies in the variety of possible income streams. Beyond simple "buy and hold" tactics, crypto lets users put assets to work. Staking, often on networks like Ethereum or Solana, allows you to lock up coins to help validate transactions while earning returns. DeFi applications allow for lending out your crypto or providing liquidity to trading pairs, earning interest or a share of transaction fees. Even the world of NFTs (non-fungible tokens) offers artists and creators the possibility of collecting royalties every time their digital work changes hands. These options mean that earning with crypto is active, not just dependent on future price swings.

Direct asset control is another powerful motivator. With crypto, you can hold your funds without relying on a bank or investment company. Only you hold the private keys to your digital wallet, and only you decide when and how to move your assets. There are no account freezes because of third-party suspicion or arbitrary withdrawal limits. For people in places where financial surveillance is strict or capital controls are routine, this kind of autonomy offers more than convenience; it can protect savings and personal freedom.

Those who join early in a changing landscape often catch new opportunities before the world catches up. Crypto is still a young market, full of innovation. Today's users can be the first to benefit from new digital assets, automated contracts that run themselves (smart contracts), and decentralized apps that deliver services in novel ways. Early adopters have at times seen rewards not just in price growth but also in shaping how technology is built and used.

Getting involved in crypto equips investors to spot real chances for growing wealth, tell safe tools apart from scams, and build strategies that match their own risk comfort and ambitions. By understanding these changes and possibilities, readers position themselves to act wisely and flexibly in the evolving world of finance.

Now that we understand how cryptocurrency differs from traditional finance by offering decentralization, transparency, and personal control, we can begin to see its true potential for transforming how we manage money and invest. This new financial landscape opens doors for anyone to participate in global markets with fewer barriers, faster transactions, and more ways to grow wealth through innovative tools like staking, lending, and digital collectibles. As you move forward, this foundational knowledge prepares you to build a smart, balanced crypto portfolio tailored to your goals—whether seeking steady income, diversification, or long-term growth while navigating the opportunities and challenges in this fast-evolving space. Embracing these changes means stepping into a future where financial freedom is more accessible and empowering than ever.

CHAPTER 2

# THE BIG TWO – INVESTING IN BITCOIN AND ETHEREUM

Most people think of cryptocurrency as a wild and confusing frontier filled with hype and risk. In reality, among thousands of coins, two digital assets, **Bitcoin** and **Ethereum**, stand out as the foundational pillars of this new financial landscape. They are not just popular names; they represent two distinct approaches to money and technology, each with its own strengths and challenges that every investor should understand.

This chapter takes a closer look at Bitcoin and Ethereum, exploring what gives them value, how they function, and what risks they carry. You will also learn practical ways to include these core assets in your portfolio so you can find the right balance between security and growth as you build your crypto investments thoughtfully. Whether you are drawn to stability and proven value or want exposure to cutting-edge innovation, understanding these two giants will give you the clarity and confidence to move forward.

## Bitcoin vs. Ethereum: Core Value, Technology, and Investment Characteristics

Bitcoin's rise started in 2009 with a single idea: create digital money that nobody could control or shut down. Satoshi Nakamoto, the anonymous creator, wrote a set of rules that all Bitcoin users follow. A big part of this design is scarcity; there will never be more than 21 million bitcoins. Think of it like a digital version of gold: there is only so much, you can't make more, and that makes each piece more valuable if enough people want it. This capped supply stands in sharp contrast to government-issued currency, which central banks regularly print in large amounts. When currencies lose value due to inflation or economic turbulence, Bitcoin attracts people who want to protect the value of their money.

The technology behind Bitcoin is the blockchain - a public, transparent record of every movement of coins. Each transaction joins a secure chain of data shared by thousands of computers all over the world. Nobody needs to ask permission to use Bitcoin, which makes it censorship-resistant. No single government, company, or person can freeze your coins or block your payments. These qualities draw investors who fear instability or restrictions in traditional finance.

People sometimes call Bitcoin "digital gold" because, like precious metals, it acts as a store of value. Throughout history, gold has helped people hedge against inflation, government takeovers, and global shocks. Public companies like MicroStrategy and Tesla invest in Bitcoin, hoping it will outlast cash's volatility. El Salvador moved even further, adopting Bitcoin as legal tender and allowing people to use it for everyday payments alongside the U.S. dollar. Large investors and small savers alike treat Bitcoin as a secure boat in stormy economic seas.

A Bitcoin transaction works without intermediaries. When you send coins, your request is broadcast to the entire network. Miners, which are powerful computers, compete to verify and add your payment to the blockchain. This process rewards them with small amounts of newly created bitcoin, but the total supply will never exceed twenty-one million coins. Because every transaction is public and the system relies on mathematics rather than human trust or government control, long-term investors view Bitcoin as both reliable and secure.

Bitcoin's primary role is security and preservation of value, which makes it a favorite among those who prioritize stability over speculation. However, not everyone in the crypto world wants to simply hold their coins and wait for growth. This is where Ethereum enters, with a broader and more dynamic vision.

Ethereum, created by Vitalik Buterin and launched in 2015, was designed to do more than just move money. It introduced the idea of a programmable blockchain. This allows developers to write code, known as smart contracts, that lives directly on the blockchain and runs automatically without human oversight or intermediaries. The simplest way to understand a smart contract is to imagine a vending machine. You insert a coin, the machine checks the amount, and it instantly delivers the correct item—no negotiation or trust required. On Ethereum, this same logic applies to more complex actions, such as lending money, operating marketplaces, or tracking ownership of digital artwork.

Ethereum now forms the backbone of what many call the decentralized web, or Web3. Here, anyone can create and use applications that operate beyond the control of traditional companies. Examples include decentralized finance (DeFi) platforms, where people lend and borrow money using only code, with no banks involved. Decentralized exchanges like Uniswap allow users to trade cryptocurrency directly with one another at any time of day. Ethereum also opened the door to NFTs, or non-fungible tokens, which represent digital art, collectibles, and other unique assets recorded on the blockchain. Because these ownership records cannot be changed or erased, NFTs have created entirely new markets for creativity and digital property.

Ethereum remains flexible because its community constantly upgrades and improves the network. Exciting changes such as the shift from proof-of-work to proof-of-stake make Ethereum more energy-efficient and allow investors to earn rewards by locking up coins for a period (called staking). This ability to evolve keeps Ethereum at the front of blockchain innovations.

Comparing Bitcoin to Ethereum shows two powerful but different anchors in crypto. Bitcoin stands as the secure, predictable store of value, more like a digital safe than a playground for invention. Its main risks involve regulatory changes, price swings, and rare software upgrades. For example, sudden government bans or harsh regulations can cause Bitcoin's price to drop sharply, but many times it recovers as broader acceptance returns.

Ethereum carries more risk but more room for growth. Changes to the protocol, such as past hard forks or the move to staking, can push prices up or down quickly. Regulatory uncertainty affects its DeFi and NFT applications. Yet projects running on Ethereum can grow rapidly; DeFi alone grew from almost nothing to billions of dollars in assets in just a couple of years.

Understanding the differences between Bitcoin and Ethereum helps you answer a simple question: what do you expect and want from crypto? Some will use Bitcoin's safety to guard against inflation. Others will put their energy into Ethereum's fast-growing apps. Knowing the story behind each asset helps you match your investments to your goals and leaves you ready to build a portfolio designed for both security and dynamism.

## Allocating and Investing: Practical Steps for Beginners

There's a clear logic behind focusing a starter crypto portfolio on Bitcoin and Ethereum, but the true challenge lies in deciding how these two assets fit your personal investment picture. Your split between Bitcoin and Ethereum depends on your goals and comfort as much as on each coin's qualities.

### *Step 1: Know Your Goals and Risk Preferences*

Before picking numbers, it helps to pause and think about what you want from your crypto investments. Are you looking to grow your wealth over a decade, or are you hoping for quicker gains? Does steady growth mean more to you than big upside potential, even if it means missing out on sudden highs? Everyone comes to crypto with their own priorities, and these will shape how you allocate.

#### Real-World Scenarios

- If your main focus is preserving value over the long run, perhaps you're building for retirement or just want an asset less likely to suddenly swing; tilting toward Bitcoin can offer peace of mind. Bitcoin's track record and simple use case as "digital gold" might appeal more to those with lower risk tolerance.

- If you're younger, curious, and excited by technology and growth, and you're okay with more ups and downs along the way, you may want to give Ethereum a bigger role. Its wide range of uses and faster pace of development can lead to greater returns, but also bigger drops.
- Sometimes, you simply want a steady, no-frills split for broad exposure. In this case, a basic blend can work for nearly anybody.

### *Step 2: Model Your Portfolio - Concrete Allocations*

To make these decisions practical and not just abstract, here are three sample allocations. These fit different types of investors and show how the balance shapes your experience.

• **Conservative Allocation (70% BTC, 30% ETH):**

For cautious investors who want most of their crypto dollars in what's often called the steadier coin. Imagine putting $1,000 total into crypto: you'd allocate $700 to Bitcoin and $300 to Ethereum. This setup aims to cushion big swings, making it easier to sleep at night.

• **Balanced Allocation (50% BTC, 50% ETH):**

Equal exposure to both. You get the benefits of Bitcoin's staying power and Ethereum's rapid ecosystem growth. If you want to future-proof your bet, this split gives you a foot in each world. With $2,000, you'd put $1,000 in each.

- **Growth-Focused Allocation (30% BTC, 70% ETH):**

  This strategy is ideal for investors who are chasing higher possible returns and are comfortable facing bigger price swings. Say you're investing $3,000: that makes $900 for Bitcoin and $2,100 for Ethereum. While this strategy invites more risk, it also offers a shot at stronger overall growth if Ethereum outpaces Bitcoin over time.

No split is better for everyone. These models are starting points. You can adjust for your needs. For example, if sudden losses make you anxious, stick closer to the first example. If you have a long time horizon, you can experiment with the latter.

### *Step 3: Start Investing; Simple First Steps*

Turning plans into action is where theory meets reality. It's best to make that first investment experience as smooth and secure as possible.

1. **Open an Account on a Reputable Exchange:**

   Choose a well-established exchange that supports both Bitcoin and Ethereum. Popular choices include Coinbase, Kraken, and Gemini. Set up your account, submitting verification details where required.

2. **Fund Your Account:**

   Link your bank account or debit card to deposit money. Start with an amount you're comfortable with, keeping in mind your planned allocation.

3. **Buy BTC and ETH According to Your Plan:**

Use the exchange's platform to purchase Bitcoin and Ethereum in the proportions you decided. Most places let you buy fractions, so exact amounts aren't an issue.

4. **Consider Dollar-Cost Averaging:**

Instead of buying your crypto all at once, you might prefer to buy a fixed dollar amount (like $100) each week or month. This evens out your entry price over time and avoids going all-in at a market peak.

5. **Set Up Secure Storage:**

Once purchased, move your coins to a secure digital wallet if you plan to hold them for a while. Software wallets work for small sums, while large holdings are safest in hardware wallets kept offline.

### *Step 4: Manage and Monitor Effectively*

Creating a cryptocurrency portfolio is a continuous process. Staying organized helps avoid common mistakes.

- **Rebalancing:**

Say Bitcoin grows faster and ends up at 80% of your holdings. Consider selling some to buy more Ethereum and return to your original target. Regularly check your mix every six or twelve months.

- **Risk Controls:**

Never invest what you can't afford to lose. Keep a portion of savings outside crypto for emergencies.

- **Security Basics:**

  Always enable two-factor authentication, beware of phishing links, and research any wallet or exchange before trusting it with your money.

- **Ongoing Reviews:**

  As your financial goals or confidence change, it's okay to tweak allocations. Small, thoughtful adjustments pay off more than big, panicked moves.

Step by step, this kind of approach helps develop habits that build confidence while keeping your portfolio on track.

Now that we've explored the unique strengths, risks, and real-world uses of Bitcoin and Ethereum, you're equipped to make informed decisions about how these core assets can fit your personal investment goals. Whether you seek the steady security of Bitcoin's digital gold or the exciting growth potential of Ethereum's programmable ecosystem, understanding their differences empowers you to build a portfolio that balances safety with opportunity. By thoughtfully choosing your allocations, starting with small, manageable steps, and staying engaged with regular reviews, you set yourself up for a smarter, more confident journey into crypto investing. With this foundation, you're ready to take action and grow your wealth in a way that fits your needs and embraces the future of finance.

# CHAPTER 3
# ALTCOINS AND HIDDEN GEMS

Have you ever wondered what lies beyond Bitcoin in the vast and ever-changing world of cryptocurrency? How can you tell which projects truly have potential and which are driven by hype or hidden risks? Many investors feel both curious and cautious when it comes to altcoins, the digital currencies that promise innovation but often come with uncertainty. What makes some altcoins rise as valuable investments while others fade into obscurity or even lead to losses?

If you have experimented with crypto before but want to take a smarter, more strategic approach, you are not alone. This chapter will guide you through the many different types of altcoins, how to evaluate their real worth, and how to protect yourself from common mistakes as you explore this exciting and unpredictable part of the market.

## Understanding Altcoins: Types, Categories, and Major Players

In the world of cryptocurrency, altcoins include everything beyond Bitcoin. Some people treat Ethereum as its own category because of its size and influence, but technically it is an altcoin too. Altcoins span hundreds of different digital coins and tokens, each created for a unique purpose that often goes beyond simple payments. When you hear the term "altcoin," think of a fast-moving landscape filled with ideas, communities, and businesses all competing to redefine what money, platforms, or digital ownership can be.

Altcoins can be grouped into several categories based on their main functions. Payment coins, such as Litecoin and Monero, work as forms of digital cash, focusing on fast, low-cost, and secure transfers. Platform tokens, including Ethereum and Solana, act as the fuel that powers entire ecosystems, enabling decentralized apps, smart contracts, and even the creation of new tokens. Utility tokens serve a specific function or provide access to a service rather than just transferring value. For example, Chainlink is used to deliver trusted data to smart contracts.

Stablecoins take a different approach. By linking their value to real-world currencies like the US dollar, coins such as USDC or Tether aim to offer stability during volatile market conditions. Finally, governance tokens, like UNI from Uniswap, allow holders to vote on project updates and future decisions, giving users a direct voice in how the platform evolves.

## Ways Altcoins Get Grouped

Investors pay close attention to how coins are grouped because these categories directly influence both risk and opportunity. Market capitalization, or market cap, remains the classic first filter. It is calculated by multiplying a token's price by the number of coins in circulation. Some of the largest altcoins by market cap include Ethereum (ETH) and Binance Coin (BNB). Because of their size and established track records, these tend to carry lower risk than smaller or newly launched tokens.

Another key factor is technological purpose. "Layer 1" coins such as Avalanche (AVAX), Cardano (ADA), and Solana (SOL) operate their own decentralized blockchains, serving as the foundation for apps, tokens, and entire projects. "Layer 2" tokens, by contrast, are built on top of major chains like Ethereum to improve transaction speed or reduce costs.

Altcoins can also be grouped by sector to help investors identify focus areas. DeFi tokens, such as AAVE and COMP, power decentralized lending and borrowing platforms. NFT ecosystem coins, including Axie Infinity Shards (AXS) and Decentraland (MANA), support gaming, virtual worlds, and digital collectibles. Some projects bridge multiple categories, but understanding their primary sector provides context and makes it easier to evaluate their purpose.

These distinctions matter because each category carries a different balance of risk and reward. A portfolio filled with small-cap NFT coins will likely rise and fall sharply with trends, while one that includes larger "layer 1" assets or stablecoins will behave more steadily. Knowing where each altcoin fits helps investors build balanced portfolios and avoid concentrating too much risk in one type of project.

## Major Altcoins and Their Innovations

Some altcoins have taken center stage through popularity or new technology. Ethereum's network introduced "smart contracts," small programs that run exactly as programmed, forming the core of DeFi and NFTs. Investors use ETH for everything from running decentralized exchanges to launching collectibles. On another front, Binance Smart Chain (BNB) cuts transaction costs and processes trades quickly, making it a favorite for low-fee users. Solana is widely known for speed and the ability to handle thousands of transactions per second. Builders often select Solana for apps needing low fees and fast updates. Cardano offers a more academic approach, basing changes on research and peer reviews, which attracts those looking for something reliable and carefully managed.

Beyond payments, altcoins spark new growth areas: decentralized finance, digital voting, blockchain gaming, and linking real data to the blockchain for smart contracts. These shifts show that investing in altcoins taps into more than just currency—it's a way to access technology trends early.

## Researching Altcoins Like a Pro

Finding the gold among altcoins demands careful research and professional skepticism. Start with the project's whitepaper, which explains the technology, goals, and token distribution. A strong whitepaper should be clear and detailed, outlining the use case and how the token works. Next, check out the team. Who are the founders and developers? Do they list real names and profiles? Is there an active developer community on GitHub? Frequent code updates are a sign a project is alive and improving.

Tokenomics gives clues about supply, demand, and distribution: Is the supply fixed? How are new coins released? Does the team have a huge stash, or is ownership widely shared? Security and audits matter here. Has the project been checked by trusted third-party auditors? Have any bugs or hacks happened, and if so, how were they handled?

Explore community activity. Lively chats on Twitter, Discord, or Reddit, and clear communication from the project team, point to a vibrant ecosystem. Double-check credible industry news. A loud social media presence with little substance often means hype is running ahead of progress.

Consider an example. Suppose you're looking at a new DeFi token. The whitepaper sounds exciting, but GitHub shows barely any code updates, and the founders are anonymous. Red flag. In contrast, a project like Chainlink has open development, frequent code pushes, and major integrations. This suggests substance over hype without making a judgment call to buy.

A huge world of coins brings both fresh ideas and real dangers. With so many new tokens launching, research skills keep you ahead of hype and scams, setting you up to handle even higher-risk corners of the crypto universe.

## Navigating Small-Cap Coins and Avoiding Risks

When you step beyond established altcoins, the landscape becomes far less predictable. The stakes rise quickly. In this space, small-cap coins and so-called hidden gems promise fortune while concealing plenty of traps. Early-stage tokens have turned ordinary investors into millionaires overnight. New ideas, overlooked use cases, and low entry prices often tempt bold investors eager to catch the next major trend just as it begins. These projects sometimes thrive by addressing needs that larger coins overlook. For example, one coin built to help small businesses send global payments grew from pennies to dollars in a matter of weeks after a wave of users sought cheaper transactions. Another focused on NFT ticketing found rapid adoption as artists and venues searched for new ways to earn revenue. Stories like these fuel the excitement and sense of possibility that surround emerging coins.

Not every small-cap story ends well. In fact, most do not. The same qualities that make these coins appealing—newness, niche innovation, and early-stage markets—also make them risky. For every project that succeeds, countless others fade away or vanish entirely. Small-cap coins are known for extreme price swings that go far beyond what large tokens experience. Gains of 100 percent in a week can be followed by a total collapse the next. Because trading volume is low, even one large buy or sell can send prices soaring or crashing in seconds.

The dangers extend beyond volatility. Small-cap coins often attract scams, manipulation, and quick-profit schemes. One of the most common is the pump and dump. This occurs when a person or group hypes up a low-value coin using social media, chat groups, or fake news to create buzz. As more investors rush in, prices surge and appear unstoppable. Meanwhile, the promoters quietly plan their exit. Once enough new buyers have entered, they sell their holdings all at once, sending the price into free fall. Those who arrived late are left holding coins worth a fraction of what they paid. These scams thrive because oversight is limited and it is easy to fabricate online enthusiasm.

Spotting danger before you get caught takes a watchful eye and a clear routine. Warning signs rarely appear in isolation, and a single red flag is enough reason to pause or walk away. Some of the most common indicators include:

- **Thin trading volume:** If only a few trades happen each day, it means there is little demand. In a rush, you could find yourself unable to sell at any price. For example, a new coin might show wild price movements and huge percentage gains on small trades, but trying to cash out even a modest sum crashes the price.
- **Anonymous or unverifiable team:** Projects run by people with fake names or no history should set off alarms. If you cannot find details about the founders, or if the team has no public presence, there is no reason to trust them. For instance, a "world-changing" coin surfaced with a slick website and an active Telegram but offered only cartoon avatars for team bios.
- **Vague or plagiarized whitepapers:** A whitepaper that repeats buzzwords, copies content from other projects, or never quite explains why this coin matters is a bad sign. In one case, a supposedly "innovative" coin had a whitepaper that was nearly identical to older projects—change a logo here and there, but no original thinking underneath.
- **Excessive social media hype:** If most mentions of a coin come from paid promotions, spammy influencers, or viral "pump" campaigns, there's a good chance the buzz is artificial. An example is when a Twitter account with fake followers spends days promising huge returns with no clear reason why the price should rise.

- **Misleading partnerships or endorsements:** Some projects will claim to be tied to big brands or celebrities, but closer inspection falls apart. For example, a coin claimed a deal with a major payment processor, but the processor denied any link when asked.
- **Unclear token utility:** If you can't figure out what problem the token solves—or if the use case feels forced—it's likely just a vehicle for speculation. As one coin advertised "the future of finance," its actual function was just to trade back and forth with no real-world purpose.

Moving with caution means acting on these signals. Always run background checks on anyone connected to the project. Examine a project's GitHub or similar code repository to see if development is ongoing or stale. Verify that liquidity is available by checking reputable exchanges, not just obscure platforms. Review third-party research from sources that are independent and not paid to promote. Solid skepticism is a must. If something feels off, walk away; there is no shame in safety.

Avoid FOMO at all costs. Set a personal checklist before every new investment. Step back for hours, or even days, before putting money at risk. Some investors use demo accounts or simulated trades to test if their reasoning holds up under less pressure. These habits put your future back in your hands. Every move in small-cap coins should start with one question: What am I risking, and why? Staying safe means making sure the answer is always clear.

Now that you understand the diverse world of altcoins—their types, innovations, and risks—you are better prepared to spot valuable projects and steer clear of common pitfalls. With careful research, a healthy dose of skepticism, and a clear strategy, you can confidently navigate this fast-changing market and build a crypto portfolio that balances opportunity with safety. As you move forward, remember that staying informed and patient will help you avoid hype and scams, positioning you to take advantage of the exciting growth altcoins offer while protecting your investment goals.

# CHAPTER 4
# NFTS – INVESTING BEYOND COINS

When Sarah first heard about NFTs, she pictured digital art hanging in an online gallery, beautiful but intangible and difficult to grasp as an investment. She wondered why anyone would pay hundreds or even thousands of dollars for something that couldn't be held, touched, or easily understood, like stocks or coins. Yet stories of people earning impressive profits through NFTs kept surfacing, often alongside warnings about scams and sudden market crashes.

Confused by the mix of hype and caution, Sarah hesitated. She wasn't alone. Many investors find themselves in the same position, curious about the potential of NFTs but wary of diving in without a clear understanding of what they are, how they hold value, and what it truly takes to invest wisely.

This chapter helps navigate that uncertainty, offering a grounded look at NFTs beyond the headlines. By the end, you'll have a clear picture of how they work, what drives their value, and whether they deserve a place in your own financial strategy.

## Understanding NFTs: Definitions, Valuation, and Real-World Applications

NFTs represent digital items that exist as unique entries on a blockchain, a shared digital ledger that records who owns what. The key word, non-fungible, means that each NFT is different from every other NFT, unlike cryptocurrencies such as Bitcoin or Ethereum. For example, one Bitcoin is equal in value to another and can be exchanged without any change in worth. NFTs, on the other hand, are like trading cards or autographed sneakers. Each has its own traits, history, and story that make it one of a kind and not directly interchangeable with another.

Imagine buying a limited-edition baseball card. Only a few exist, you know exactly which one you have, and collectors may pay a premium for it. With NFTs, the same concept applies digitally and on a larger scale, but with technology that verifies who truly owns the item. When someone purchases a piece of digital art as an NFT, they gain a record of ownership stored on the blockchain. This record is public, easy to verify, and cannot be faked or erased. Owning an NFT does not always mean you own the rights to copy or sell the image itself, but it does mean you own that unique, digitally signed version. Artists can upload their work to platforms like OpenSea or Foundation, set how many editions exist, and sell them as NFTs to buyers around the world. When the sale completes, the blockchain updates with the new owner's information. If someone sells the NFT later, the blockchain tracks the transfer, so buyers never have to worry about forgeries.

The value of an NFT depends on more than just the artwork or item itself. Several factors work together to determine its worth. Rarity attracts collectors who seek something truly scarce, where only a handful of versions or perhaps just one exist. The reputation and following of the creator also play a major role. A work from Beeple, the digital artist who sold "Everydays: The First 5000 Days" at Christie's in 2021, reached 69 million dollars because of both scarcity and the artist's global recognition. The sale proved that NFTs can hold immense value when creative vision and cultural impact align.

Historical significance can also influence value. Was the NFT connected to a defining moment in technology, gaming, or art? In some cases, access adds another layer of worth, as certain NFTs grant holders ongoing benefits such as entry into exclusive communities or access to new content releases.

Social trends can shift NFT prices dramatically. When a collection captures public attention, it can evolve into a status symbol of digital ownership. The Bored Ape Yacht Club, for example, became far more than a set of digital images. Owners connected through private events, online communities, and a shared sense of identity. The excitement attracted celebrities and everyday investors alike. However, not every collection enjoys lasting success, and prices can fall sharply once the spotlight fades.

The ways people use NFTs go well beyond art collecting. Artists have found new ways to monetize digital works. Instead of selling files that can be copied endlessly, they mint NFTs and sell them in limited supply. Buyers enjoy not just bragging rights but also confidence that their purchase is genuine and recorded. Musicians, too, have begun releasing albums or concert tickets in NFT form, creating new income streams and fan engagement models. Platforms like Royal let fans buy a share of music streaming rights as NFTs.

In gaming, NFTs have created fresh economics inside virtual worlds. In Axie Infinity, a game with a booming NFT economy; players buy, sell, and breed digital creatures called "Axies." These creatures are NFTs that players actually own, trade, or use in battles. Sometimes, a rare Axie or in-game tool gains real-world value, with sales crossing tens of thousands of dollars. Players can make money by selling what they earn or find in the game, blurring old lines between entertainment and investing.

NFTs also serve in membership and rewards. Groups like Proof Collective or VeeFriends grant NFT holders access to closed communities, network events, or annual conferences. Instead of a printed card, members show their digital wallet as their ticket. This approach helps clubs prove membership quickly and add features over time, such as special content or meetups for NFT owners only.

Ongoing experiments in utility NFTs are changing ticketing and event access. Some companies now issue event passes as NFTs. The owner can resell a ticket safely, because the blockchain proves authenticity and prevents duplication. The original event organizer can even take a share of any resale, a trick that fights scalping and rewards creators.

These examples show both the creative energy and new risks in NFT markets. Ownership, authenticity, hype, and utility mix together, shaping a fast-moving landscape that attracts attention and speculation. NFT investing offers possibilities but demands careful planning. With this foundation, investors can start to think through how to approach NFTs: whether to flip, hold, or seek long-term value, and how to stay safe as they do.

## Investment Strategies and Risk Management in NFTs

A solid foundation in NFT concepts paves the way for safer, more confident investing. Before making any moves, it's smart to recognize the unique risks of the NFT space. NFT markets move quickly and attract opportunists. Some projects may disappear overnight, and not all marketplaces offer equal security. Start by sticking to well-known marketplaces like OpenSea, Rarible, or LooksRare, which have established tools and clear user protections. Double-check that any NFT project's creator profile is verified, and look for links to recognized social accounts. Before purchasing, examine smart contract details; public block explorers let you review contract addresses, verify conditions, and spot irregularities.

Community reputation can signal a project's health. Read feedback in Discords, Telegram groups, and Twitter replies. Watch for accounts with only a few posts or sudden boosts in followers; these are red flags for artificial hype. Search for independent reviews or trackers that assess project milestones or reveal past troubles. Always set spending limits and separate funds used for NFT purchases from the money you need for bills or daily expenses. Even the most promising projects carry risk, so only invest what you can afford to lose.

Emotions play a big role in NFT investing. FOMO spikes during high-profile drops, often leading to hurried buying without proper research. Pause before making decisions; even a short wait can prevent regret. Instances of poorly researched projects abound: in some cases, teams promised unique artwork or rare perks, launched with flashy websites, and then vanished after the initial sale. Compare that to buyers who thoroughly checked team backgrounds, confirmed digital signatures, chatted with other collectors, and saw stable project progress; these investments are more likely to grow in value or at least avoid disaster.

Short-term flipping offers a way to profit by buying and selling NFTs in quick succession. This strategy hinges on timing and finding collections primed for attention. Ideal flipping candidates often have limited supply, strong buzz across social media, or feature highly anticipated timed drops. Flippers typically monitor Discord and Twitter for early signs of community excitement, often using NFT analytics tools like Nansen or Icy Tools to spot trending projects. They track mint dates, whitelist opportunities, and pre-sale leaks.

In a typical flipping scenario, an investor sees a surge of genuine chatter about an upcoming collection. By analyzing recent engagement and activity levels, the investor joins before the general public. If they secure an NFT at mint price, they list it for resale at the first peak of interest, sometimes within hours. Gas fees (transaction costs on the Ethereum network) can eat into profits, so flippers monitor network congestion and set firm price targets to keep trades worthwhile.

Flipping is not without its pitfalls. Prices can plunge just as quickly as they rise, locking up funds in unwanted NFTs. Slow secondary sales may also mean assets cannot be liquidated in time. By setting entry and exit rules, flippers can minimize chasing sudden shifts, and calculating costs in advance helps them avoid unprofitable trades.

Some investors lean toward holding NFTs over longer periods, believing that certain collections or items will increase in value slowly but steadily. Long-term strategies focus on assets with meaningful utility, established creators, and highly engaged communities. NFTs tied to game economies, recurring member perks, or evolving digital art often see gradual and sustained appreciation. Buyers dive into project roadmaps, check the professional credentials of the development team, and watch for regular updates or expanding perks.

The quality of art, development of features, and growth of exclusive benefits contribute strongly to an NFT's future appeal. Holding early in projects like CryptoPunks or Bored Ape Yacht Club allowed collectors to benefit from rising collector interest and added member experiences. These gains were not immediate but built over months, even years, as communities flourished and teams continued to deliver.

Patient analysis is vital before committing to long-term holds. Study how project goals align with delivery, and make sure the creators communicate transparently. Some long-term investors split their portfolio, reserving a portion for blue-chip NFTs and another for newer speculative projects with strong teams.

Comparing flipping and holding, the two approaches serve different types of investors. Flipping demands constant research, a quick reaction to trends, and an appetite for high risk and transaction fees. The rewards can be immediate, but losses come just as fast. Holding needs in-depth vetting, long-term patience, and a willingness to wait for value to emerge. It may carry less day-to-day stress but asks for trust in a project's ongoing life.

Think honestly about your own risk tolerance, time, and financial plans. If rapid trading suits your style and you can accept swift ups and downs, flipping could work for you. If you'd rather bet on the steady rise of carefully chosen projects, long-term holding may fit better. Blending both approaches or starting small with one can allow for learning and growth without overextending, making NFT investing a more controlled and informed process.

Now that you understand the core ideas behind NFTs, their uniqueness, value factors, and range of uses, you are better prepared to decide whether they fit into your investment strategy. NFTs offer exciting opportunities but also carry distinct risks in a market that evolves quickly. Whether you aim for short-term profits or long-term growth, success depends on careful research and a clear plan. By staying objective, verifying projects thoroughly, and aligning your strategy with your goals and risk tolerance, you can navigate the NFT world with confidence and build a crypto portfolio that supports your path to financial freedom.

# CHAPTER 5
# WALLETS, EXCHANGES, AND TOOLS YOU NEED

Have you ever wondered how to safely buy and store cryptocurrency without falling prey to scams or losing your assets? Are you unsure whether to use a centralized platform that feels more familiar or a decentralized option that offers greater control? Maybe you're curious about which tools can help you track your investments and protect your digital wealth as the market moves rapidly. These are common questions for anyone stepping into the world of crypto, especially when the choices seem overwhelming and the risks real.

This chapter will guide you through the essential decisions and tools needed to build a strong foundation in cryptocurrency investing. You'll learn about different types of exchanges and wallets, how each fits various goals and comfort levels, and practical steps to secure your holdings. We'll also explore helpful apps for tracking your portfolio and staying informed, along with best practices to keep your investments safe from threats. By the end, you'll have a clearer understanding of the must-have resources and security habits that make confident, smart crypto investing possible.

## Exchanges and Secure Wallet Choices

Centralized and decentralized exchanges shape how you buy, sell, and hold cryptocurrency. Understanding the difference between these two options is the first step to making informed decisions about your portfolio.

A centralized exchange, or CEX, works a bit like a crypto bank. You sign up for an account, usually with a photo ID and personal information. The platform holds your funds, matches buyers and sellers, and lets you trade digital assets for fiat currency or other cryptocurrencies with the click of a button. Trusted names in the CEX space include Coinbase, Binance, and Kraken. These platforms make it easy to deposit dollars, euros, or other traditional currencies, which can streamline your first steps into crypto.

Centralized exchanges often appeal to new investors because of their user-friendly design, strong customer support, and sense of familiarity. These platforms hold your crypto for you, so you don't have to worry about managing keys or backup phrases right away. High trading volume means you can usually buy or sell quickly, even during busy market hours. CEXs are heavily regulated, so they follow regional laws on consumer protection and anti-money laundering. That comes with the trade-off of personal identity disclosure, account monitoring, and sometimes account freezes.

Decentralized exchanges, or DEXs, trade all that structure for freedom. DEXs are peer-to-peer marketplaces, closer to a neighborhood swap meet than a bank. You trade directly with other users through your own crypto wallet, and there's no central company holding your funds or collecting your identity. Popular DEXs include Uniswap and PancakeSwap. They're accessible through an internet browser or mobile app, connecting directly to blockchain networks like Ethereum or Binance Smart Chain.

DEXs give you more control and privacy. You don't have to register with your name or email, instead, you link your own wallet and start trading. These platforms often carry new or rare coins that never make it to big exchanges. The flip side is that you're responsible for securing your own funds and navigating sometimes complicated user interfaces. Transaction fees can spike during busy periods, and support typically comes from the community rather than a help desk.

Choosing between a CEX and a DEX depends on your comfort with technology, privacy priorities, and tolerance for risk:

**When to consider a CEX:**

- You want an easy start with fiat money
- You value customer support and strong account security features
- You trade large amounts or need high liquidity

**When a DEX might fit you better:**

- You want privacy and personal control
- You're interested in hard-to-find coins
- You're willing to manage your own wallet security and accept responsibility for mistakes

Wallets are the next foundation. In crypto, a wallet is where you store your digital keys, which are required to access your assets. Every wallet type has trade-offs, and picking the right one depends on what you value most: convenience, security, or long-term safety.

Hot wallets connect to the internet. They come as browser extensions, mobile apps, or desktop programs. Examples include MetaMask, Trust Wallet, and Coinbase Wallet. Hot wallets are convenient for daily trading, especially for people who frequently buy and sell coins and want to react quickly to market changes. They make moving funds simple but also expose users to hacks, scams, and device theft. Keeping large sums in a hot wallet increases risk. There are many stories of investors who lost all their crypto through phishing attacks or malware because their wallets remained connected online.

Cold wallets store your crypto keys offline. The simplest version is a paper wallet, which is just a printed document with your key codes. More common are hardware wallets, small USB-like devices such as Ledger and Trezor. They remain offline except when plugged in to sign a transaction, eliminating most online threats. Hardware wallets offer the best balance between accessibility and security for serious investors. Some people have lost access to exchanges but recovered their funds using a hardware backup, while others lost everything because they kept their crypto online.

Before choosing a wallet, consider three things: control of your private keys (are you the only one who has them?), backup options (can you recover your wallet if your computer fails?), and security features such as two-factor authentication or passphrase protection.

A strong foundation built on reliable exchanges and wallets forms the base for everything you do in crypto. Once you have these in place, adding tools like tracking apps, tax software, or portfolio analytics becomes easier and safer. Each layer adds both strength and flexibility, beginning with how and where you store and trade your assets.

## Essential Crypto Tools and Security Practices

Everyday crypto investors depend on a range of tools to keep track of markets, manage assets, spot fraud, and maintain control. One of the first essentials in any toolkit is a trusted market data aggregator. For this purpose, sites like CoinMarketCap and CoinGecko exist. With these resources, you can look up any coin, check real-time prices, and compare trading volumes and liquidity across exchanges. Each site lets you dig deeper by showing market cap rankings, historical charts, project summaries, and links to official websites or contract addresses. This makes it simple to avoid lookalike coins or scam tokens with similar names.

Setting price alerts on these sites is a practical step. Imagine seeing a sudden price pump on social media; a quick check on CoinGecko helps you see actual changes, price history, volume patterns, and whether the move is happening across major exchanges or just one illiquid spot. If you're waiting to buy or sell, these tools' alert systems let you set target prices. You'll get a push notification or email the moment your conditions are met, rather than reacting impulsively to headlines or FOMO (fear of missing out).

Portfolio tracker apps are another must-have. With dozens of coins and wallets, you need a clear snapshot of everything you own. Apps like Blockfolio or Delta connect directly to your wallets and exchanges. Instead of logging in to five separate accounts, you see all your balances, total net worth, and performance charts in one place. This ease is useful during wild market swings. For example, when Bitcoin declines by 15% overnight and you want to see your overall exposure or how your altcoins are holding up, a tracker app answers instantly.

Many portfolio trackers offer more than just basic summaries. Look for features like automatic price updating, built-in tax reports, and detailed charts showing unrealized gains and losses. When tax season arrives, a tracker with an integrated reporting tool can save days of frustration. All transfers, swaps, and trades are logged automatically if you connect your wallets using public 'read-only' keys or APIs. No need to share private keys or give up security.

## Setting Up Tracking and Research Tools

Here's a short step-by-step guide to integrating trackers and data sources:

1. Download a portfolio app from the official website or app store.
2. Choose the 'add wallet' or 'add exchange' option.
3. If the app supports wallet syncing, paste in your public (not private) wallet address.
4. For exchange syncing, log in using a secure 'read-only' API key, never a withdrawal-enabled one.
5. Assign a name to the app, and observe as it automatically imports balances and trades.
6. Set price alerts for coins you follow.
7. Activate two-factor authentication on the app.

For market research, aggregators like Messari or CryptoPanic combine news headlines, project updates, and even developer activity. You see the source and timestamp for every alert. When rumors break, these platforms let you verify news with a single glance. On-chain analytics sites like Glassnode reveal investor behavior, large wallet movements, and unusual activity, signaling possible pump-and-dump schemes.

Social media monitoring also matters. Crypto markets move on tweets and Reddit threads. Aggregators filter the noise by pulling key updates or sometimes warning of coordinated 'shilling' campaigns. By collecting news from official Twitter or Medium feeds, these tools help you distinguish between real project announcements and viral rumors.

## Security Best Practices

Security is the foundation for protecting your investments. Start with strong, unique passwords for each exchange, wallet, and app. Use a password manager like Bitwarden or 1Password, which generates and remembers complex passwords so you don't reuse the same one.

Always enable two-factor authentication (2FA). Google Authenticator or Authy is the gold standard here. Authentication by SMS is vulnerable to SIM swapping, so stick with app-based codes. Every login and transfer should prompt for this second code, making it almost impossible for a hacker to access your account with only your password.

Only download wallet software, portfolio apps, and extensions from official download links or recognized app stores. Fake apps or malicious browser add-ons are a common trick; a single download can steal your coins.

Phishing attacks are common, so check every website address before entering passwords. Bookmark important sites, and ignore suspicious emails or direct messages offering unexpected giveaways or claiming wallet issues. Never share backup phrases or private keys, not even with customer support.

## Backup Strategies

Losing access to a wallet can mean losing everything. Keep written backup phrases in a safe offline location (never digital notes or cloud storage). Use password managers to store exchange logins, but store wallet seed phrases on paper or a hardware device, separate from your computer.

If you use multi-signature wallets or hardware wallets, keep backup devices or written instructions in different safe locations. Let a trusted family member know where the backup is, just in case.

In volatile or uncertain times, these practices help remove stress from investing. A security mistake or app failure feels far less frightening when you have reliable backups and trusted tools in place. Tools work best when combined with disciplined habits, helping you avoid panic, scams, and unnecessary losses while giving you the confidence to grow and protect your crypto wealth.

Now that you understand the key choices between exchanges and wallets, along with the essential tools and security habits needed to manage your crypto safely, you're ready to take confident steps into this dynamic market. Building a strong foundation means you can focus on growing your portfolio without fear of common pitfalls like scams or lost assets. With these basics in place, you can explore advanced strategies to diversify your holdings, track your progress effectively, and protect your investments with smart backups and alerts. This chapter sets the stage for you to move forward thoughtfully and securely, turning curiosity into real financial opportunity in the world of cryptocurrency.

CHAPTER 6

# BUILDING A PROFITABLE CRYPTO PORTFOLIO

Many people jump into cryptocurrency expecting quick wins, only to find themselves caught in a rollercoaster of unpredictable prices and risky bets. The truth is, building real wealth with crypto isn't about chasing the latest hype or betting everything on one coin. It requires a thoughtful strategy that balances growth potential with risk management, especially in a market known for wild swings.

This chapter will guide you through creating a crypto portfolio designed for steady, methodical wealth growth. You'll learn how to combine reliable core assets with carefully chosen satellites to match your comfort level with risk. We'll explore practical ways to diversify across coins and sectors, use different investment methods, and manage your holdings over time. By the end, you'll have a clear plan tailored to your financial goals—whether you want conservative stability or are ready to take bigger chances while protecting your capital.

## Understanding Portfolio Foundations: Core and Satellite Assets with Sample Strategies

A strong crypto portfolio does not rely on a single asset or short-term hunches. Investors use a smart approach called core-satellite investing to structure their holdings for both growth and stability. This strategy divides your assets into two types. The core forms the backbone, made up of the largest and most established cryptocurrencies such as Bitcoin and Ethereum. Satellite assets surround the core and include altcoins, DeFi tokens, NFTs, and newer projects that carry higher risk. Grouping your investments in this way allows you to pursue growth while protecting your capital from the sharp fluctuations of the crypto market.

Core assets hold a key place in this structure because of their history and broad acceptance. Bitcoin is recognized as the first and most widely adopted cryptocurrency, known for its limited supply and strong network effects. Ethereum serves as the main platform for smart contracts and decentralized applications, forming the base for much of the innovation in the crypto space today. Both have survived multiple market cycles, proving their durability and importance within the broader digital economy. Holding a healthy share of your portfolio in such coins means you are anchored to assets with solid liquidity, brand recognition, and ongoing developer support.

Satellite assets, on the other hand, introduce excitement and potential for quick gains, but with them comes more risk. These assets include well-known altcoins beyond Bitcoin and Ethereum, smaller network coins, tokens powering specific dApps, and even collectibles like NFTs. Sometimes, satellites can multiply in value in a short period; think of tokens that surge after a new protocol or game draws market attention. Still, most satellites are more experimental or tied to a single trend, which makes them unpredictable. If things go wrong, you protect most of your capital by only investing a small part of your portfolio.

This division is not just for safety. It actively supports your long-term returns. Core assets can help smooth out ups and downs in the crypto market, giving you time to wait for the right moments with your satellites. If some speculative bets pay off, you have room to lock in profits and cycle gains back into your core, strengthening your base over time. If satellites dip or fail, your core can prevent the entire portfolio from collapsing. Altogether, you follow a plan, not a gambling streak.

## Example Portfolios for Different Risk Levels

Some investors want maximum stability and steady growth. For a conservative profile, a portfolio might look like this:

**Core (80%)**

- 50% Bitcoin (BTC)
- 30% Ethereum (ETH)

**Satellite (20%)**

- 10% Binance Coin (BNB)
- 5% Polygon (MATIC)
- 5% Chainlink (LINK)

This combination allows the core to maintain its value during challenging times, while satellites provide additional growth opportunities without jeopardizing your base wealth.

For those comfortable with more risk, preference shifts a bit:

**Core (60%)**

- 35% Bitcoin (BTC)
- 25% Ethereum (ETH)

**Satellite (40%)**

- 10% Solana (SOL)
- 10% Avalanche (AVAX)
- 10% Uniswap (UNI)
- 10% in new DeFi or metaverse projects

This kind of balance meets the needs of someone who believes in crypto's future but wants to avoid betting it all on one horse. You can tap into fresh trends and sectors while still holding fast to the strongest coins.

For those who enjoy taking bigger swings on rapid gains and are ready to handle losses, an aggressive approach might resemble the following:

**Core (40%)**

- 20% Bitcoin (BTC)
- 20% Ethereum (ETH)

**Satellite (60%)**

- 15% in trending metaverse tokens
- 15% in small-cap altcoins with growth buzz
- 10% in early-stage DeFi protocols
- 10% in select NFTs
- 10% in ecosystem tokens, like Fantom (FTM) or Cosmos (ATOM)

This portfolio backs up its moonshot chasing with enough core to soften a hard market crash, making it more disciplined than going "all in" on unproven coins. It draws boundaries, so even when chasing high rewards, the risk of ruin is limited.

## How Core-Satellite Investing Works During Market Shocks

Imagine an investor who held only hyped altcoins during a sharp correction, say, a 60% drop in new project prices over weeks. They could lose much of their principal and then hesitate or sell off in panic, missing the recovery. Someone using a core-satellite structure, on the other hand, might find their Bitcoin and Ethereum holdings drop too, but with much smaller drawdowns. The core assets are more likely to recover, providing a cushion, while at least some satellites might bounce strongly later, letting the investor rebalance when the storm has passed.

The concept of core and satellite provides structure and stability in a market characterized by swift fluctuations. Once this basic balance is set, another question grows: how do you pick the best satellites, and how can you make your portfolio even more resilient and full of opportunity by diversifying within those satellites? Sectors, strategies, and asset types offer many new ways forward.

## Implementing Diversification and Ongoing Management Techniques

Step-by-step portfolio construction is just the start. Maximizing returns and limiting risk come from weaving together several types of diversification and sticking with steady management methods.

Spreading risk by coin type matters for crypto more than in most markets. Lean too heavily on large coins like Bitcoin or Ethereum, and performance may mirror only market trends. If you invest all your money in small-cap coins in the hopes of achieving a significant return, the unpredictable fluctuations could potentially disrupt your goals or even completely erase your progress. The sweet spot often lies in blending these: large-cap coins for their staying power with doses of mid-cap and small-cap coins for upside potential.

A sample allocation could look like this:

- 60% in large-cap coins: Bitcoin, Ethereum
- 25% in mid-cap coins: Solana, Polygon, Avalanche
- 15% in small-cap coins: new DeFi or gaming tokens

Here, the majority sits in assets with long histories and active communities. This anchors the portfolio against sharp downturns. The mid- and small-cap slices let you tap projects at earlier stages, which are risky but offer higher growth. If something goes wrong with a small-cap, losses won't sink the whole portfolio.

Coins are only one way to diversify. Crypto spreads across sectors that behave differently as the market changes. Relying on only one segment, maybe all "layer 1" blockchains like Ethereum and its peers could leave you exposed if that sector faces trouble, such as network congestion, major hacks, or regulation. Layer 2 solutions, made to improve speed and reduce fees, do not always move in step with layer 1s. Decentralized finance (DeFi) protocols might stumble during market fear but bounce back on innovation or adoption. NFT and gaming tokens show unique cycles, often growing during wider market slumps, which provides a degree of balance.

A robust spread could cover:

- Layer 1 blockchains: Ethereum, Cardano
- Layer 2 solutions: Polygon, Optimism
- DeFi: Aave, Uniswap, Curve
- NFTs/gaming: Axie Infinity, Decentraland
- Infrastructure: Chainlink, Filecoin

When the government cracks down on DeFi lending, DeFi coins may tumble while layer 1 blockchains or NFT platforms show resilience. The opposite might happen if NFTs lose hype but financial activity on blockchains remains strong. Spreading bets means losses in one area won't always translate to losses everywhere.

Another dimension is investment methods. It's one thing to buy and hold coins. Doing only that can miss opportunities when trends shift. Adding short- or medium-term trading lets you react to market excitement or price dips. Some coins, like Ethereum or Solana, offer "staking," locking coins up to help network security and earn a yield. Others supply income through DeFi lending or yield farming. Each method has its rewards and tradeoffs.

Suppose you allocate:

- 70% to long-term holds like Bitcoin and Ethereum
- 20% to trading positions—buying mid-cap coins on price dips, selling after gains
- 10% to income: staking Cardano, lending USDC for interest

In this mix, core assets ride long-term growth, trades aim for quicker profit, and staking or lending produces extra yield regardless of price moves. If trading hits a losing streak, steady income from staking helps smooth results.

Ongoing management gives shape to these diligent choices. Portfolios drift as prices surge or dive. Left unchecked, allocations meant for balance soon become lopsided. Say Ethereum doubles and now makes up 40% instead of the planned 25%. This exposes a portfolio to higher single-asset risk. Good investors bring it back in line with "rebalancing," selling some winners and topping up laggards.

Two common, practical ways to rebalance:

- **Time-based approach**: Once every month or quarter, review allocations and adjust as needed.
- **Threshold-based approach**: Whenever an asset shifts more than, say, 5% from its target allocation, rebalance only those parts.

For example, if DeFi coins surge to 30% of your holdings (from a 20% target), sell part for stablecoins or other assets. This keeps each category in check, protects against shock losses, and lets profits from one lucky run fuel new bets elsewhere.

Managing a portfolio is not just about adding or removing coins but judging what works. Several crypto portfolio trackers allow connections to exchanges and wallets, making it much simpler to check your exposure, track gains, and log losses. Even a manual spreadsheet with columns for entry price, amount, and sector can help.

A quick review each month, checking which sectors win, which lag, and where allocations drifted, unlocks insights. Spot a coin that always drags your totals down, and you can cut it. Notice that gaming tokens rose while everything else slid? You'll see trends to catch next time, keeping you close to your goals and steering with confidence.

Now that you understand how to build a well-structured crypto portfolio using the core-satellite approach, tailored to your risk comfort and goals, you're ready to put this knowledge into practice. By balancing stable, established coins with carefully chosen growth opportunities and maintaining ongoing management like diversification and rebalancing, you can navigate the highs and lows of the crypto market with confidence and discipline. This methodical strategy protects your investment while providing opportunities for significant gains. As you move forward, remember that success in crypto investing comes from staying informed, adapting thoughtfully, and sticking to a plan, not chasing every trend. With these tools at your disposal, you can increase your wealth over time in a steady and intelligent manner.

# CHAPTER 7
# PROFIT STRATEGIES – FROM HODLING TO DAY TRADING

Profit in the world of cryptocurrency isn't about luck or timing the market perfectly, it's about understanding different approaches and aligning them with your own goals, temperament, and daily life. Many people think there's a single right way to invest: buy and hold forever or trade rapidly to chase every price move. In reality, the best strategy depends on who you are, how much time you have, and how you handle risk and stress.

This chapter explores the range of methods available, from holding assets patiently over years to actively trading based on short-term momentum, helping you find the approach that fits you best. It also offers practical guidance on managing risks, setting rules for your trades, and developing habits that protect your investments and your peace of mind. Whether you're new to crypto or ready to take your investing to the next level, these insights will help you build a plan designed for steady, sustainable profits.

## Investment Styles: HODLing vs. Active Trading Methods

Imagine a spectrum of crypto investing styles, on one end sits the quiet patience of the HODLer, and on the other, the constant motion of the momentum trader. Each path reflects a different way to interact with the chaos and opportunity of crypto markets, each with strengths and pitfalls. Choosing a method asks you to consider what matches your mindset, your life, and your goals, much more than chasing whatever strategy is trending on social media.

HODLing, a playful twist on "hold," stands for "Hold On for Dear Life." The idea is simple; buy a crypto asset you believe in and keep it for years, resisting the urge to sell during wild price swings. Like a seedling, you nurture it, knowing it may seem weak but could grow strong and useful. This approach appeals to those with demanding jobs or tight schedules, people who prefer to set things up once, then step away. The main attraction is the simplicity. There's less pressure to time the market or constantly follow price charts. It can be tax-friendly since long-term holdings usually get better treatment in many countries. On the downside, the ride can be rough. Your investment may shrink by half during market corrections, testing your patience and nerves. Opportunity cost becomes real if crypto stagnates while other markets or investments grow. The risk here isn't just market drops but the psychological toll of seeing your portfolio down double digits for months.

Swing trading sits in the middle. Think of it as catching a train partway through its journey. Instead of riding out every bump, you aim to get on and off near the peaks and valleys of shorter trends. Swing traders look for patterns such as prices bouncing between two levels or a big move beginning to slow, then open trades that last for a few days or weeks. Unlike HODLing, swing trading requires more involvement, including frequent market checks and learning to use tools like moving averages, support and resistance zones, and candlestick patterns.

The reward is the chance to profit from the smaller ups and downs without facing the full weight of major market crashes. However, this method comes with more emotional swings, since quick reversals can erase gains. It suits people who enjoy analysis, have time to review charts after work, and feel comfortable making moderately paced decisions. Imagine a lawyer who checks the market in the evening, studies a few key indicators, and makes one or two trades each month while keeping both stress and risk under control.

Trend trading stretches the timeframe further. The goal is to recognize when an asset begins moving steadily in one direction and stay with that trend until signs of change appear. It's like following a river's current, letting the flow carry you instead of fighting every turn. Trend traders create clear rules, such as buying only when the price stays above a certain moving average or selling when specific indicators turn negative. This approach reduces the noise and stress of short-term movements. It requires patience but also alertness, since the market can sometimes trick traders with false reversals. People with steady routines, such as teachers, often prefer this style because it allows them to check the market once a day, hold positions for weeks or months, and avoid the fast pace of daily trading.

Momentum trading sits at the other end of the spectrum. Momentum traders look for coins that are already moving quickly and jump in to ride the surge, aiming to sell before the momentum fades. Imagine surfing; you have to paddle hard, catch the wave at the right moment, and exit as soon as it loses strength. This strategy demands constant attention to price charts, quick decision-making, and strict loss-control rules. The potential rewards are rapid profits, but the risks are equally fast. It appeals to people who enjoy excitement, react well under pressure, and can handle volatility. Picture a freelance marketer with flexible hours, scanning the markets for sudden opportunities and thriving on the high energy of fast trades.

To narrow in on your fit, weigh your schedule, comfort with risk, stress resilience, and desire for involvement. Ask yourself:

- Do you want to check prices once a week, or does the idea of daily action attract you?
- Are you patient when money is tied up for months, or do short-term results keep you motivated?
- How well do you cope with swings in value, or the sting of selling too soon or too late?
- Do technical charts sound interesting, or do you zone out at the mention of "support levels"?

Once you've spotted your place on this spectrum, building discipline and using practical trading tools will help you lock in profits and protect yourself from big mistakes. The coming pages break down these essential strategies—stop-loss orders, risk controls, and mindset habits—to reinforce success, no matter which style you've chosen.

## Practical Steps for Safe and Sustainable Profits

Buying and selling cryptocurrency comes with risks that skilled investors recognize and control. Setting up a stop-loss is one of the most practical ways to protect yourself from sudden downturns. A stop-loss is a preset order that tells your exchange to sell an asset if its price drops below a certain level. This tool functions similarly to insurance; if the value falls below your set limit, it automatically triggers a sale, allowing you to minimize your losses without any hesitation or panic. To set a stop-loss on most crypto exchanges, first decide your threshold. For example, if you buy Bitcoin at $30,000, you might want to risk no more than 10%. You would set your stop-loss at $27,000. On many exchanges, you click 'Stop-Limit' or 'Stop Order,' input your trigger price ($27,000), and specify the quantity to sell. You can also base your stop-loss on support levels by identifying price points where an asset has "bounced back" before and placing your order just below this zone. Percentage limits protect you from emotional overreactions, while support-based stops account for market behavior. No stop-loss is perfect, but skipping this step is the surest path to letting one disastrous trade wreck your portfolio.

Emotional highs and lows often lead to poor trading decisions. Crypto markets move quickly, inviting both fear and greed. When prices drop sharply, many traders panic and sell everything. When coins surge, fear of missing out causes others to buy too late or at inflated prices. Recognizing these emotional triggers is your first line of defense. Maybe your pulse races as prices fall, or you find yourself checking charts every few minutes after a big rally. These are signs that emotion, not logic, is guiding your actions. Planning your trades in advance helps reduce this influence. Write down your entry and exit points, and keep a trading journal to record what you intended to do versus what actually happened, along with how you felt during each step. For example, if your plan is to buy Ethereum at $2,000 and sell at $2,300 but the price hits $2,400, stick to your strategy, or at least review your plan before reacting. Building this habit prevents impulsive moves that lead to regret.

Trading around the clock or monitoring assets constantly will drain your focus. Many new traders burn out quickly by spending late nights glued to screens, trapped in a cycle of stress and rushed decisions. Fatigue leads to mistakes and risky choices. Setting boundaries is essential. Limit trading to specific hours and then walk away. Schedule short breaks to reset your mind. After a tough loss or a major win, take time off to cool down. This pause helps prevent emotional reactions such as "revenge trading," when traders try to recover losses immediately. If you notice anxiety at certain times, like when the market opens, turn off notifications and check prices only at set moments, such as lunchtime or after work. Over time, these habits protect your focus, decision-making, and peace of mind.

Tax season can also catch unprepared investors off guard. Every time you sell crypto, even when exchanging one coin for another, you may trigger a taxable event. This means each transaction must be reported on your tax return. Gains fall into two categories: short term, for assets held one year or less, and long term, for those held longer than a year. Short term gains are usually taxed at your regular income rate, while long term gains often qualify for a lower rate. For example, if you buy Litecoin for $5,000 and sell it after eleven months for $6,000, you owe short term capital gains tax on the $1,000 profit. Holding for thirteen months could qualify for a lower rate. Frequent trading increases the number of transactions and receipts to track, so using crypto tax software or hiring a professional can help prevent costly errors and audits. Staying organized from the beginning makes tax time far less stressful.

Building wealth through crypto should not look or feel like a casino trip. Gambling means chasing quick wins, ignoring losses, and making impulsive "all-in" bets. Successful investors do the opposite. They pick a small set of coins, research carefully, and set clear entry and exit rules for every trade. They use stop-losses as guardrails. Realistic expectations matter, aiming for steady, small gains and seeing losses as learning tools. Start by selecting one or two coins, not ten. Decide when you're willing to enter a trade, where your exit and stop-loss should be, and how much risk is comfortable for your finances. Track every trade in a notebook or app. Over time, review your patterns and adjust. Small, consistent efforts build into solid results, protecting you from both wild swings and burnout. The goal is control, not chance. By committing to these steps, you set yourself up for progress that lasts.

Now that you understand the spectrum of crypto investing from steady HODLing to active momentum trading and the tools to manage risk and emotions, you're equipped to choose a strategy that fits your lifestyle and goals. Remember, success comes from discipline, clear planning, and learning from each trade, not from chasing quick wins or following hype. As you move forward, keep refining your approach with practical habits like setting stop-losses, limiting stress, and staying organized for taxes. With this foundation, you can confidently build a balanced crypto portfolio designed for sustainable growth and long-term wealth.

CHAPTER 8

# PASSIVE INCOME IN CRYPTO – STAKING, YIELD FARMING & MORE

Have you ever wondered how people turn their cryptocurrency holdings into steady streams of income without constantly buying and selling? What if your digital coins could work quietly in the background, earning rewards while you focus on other things? If the idea of making money from crypto sounds exciting but confusing, you're not alone. Many investors are curious about ways to generate passive income through blockchain technology but hesitate because the landscape feels complicated and risky. Knowing where to start, which strategies are effective, and how to avoid common pitfalls can significantly impact the difference between missed opportunities and intelligent growth. This chapter will help you see how practical crypto income methods fit together, revealing paths that suit your goals and comfort level so you can build a more confident approach to earning with digital assets.

## Getting Started with Staking, Yield Farming, Lending Platforms, and Liquidity Pools

Staking opens a door for crypto holders to make their coins work for them. By locking up, or "staking," coins on certain blockchains, users help secure the network and earn regular rewards in return. Imagine someone with 10 Solana tokens. Instead of keeping them idle, they deposit these Solana into a platform like Kraken or Coinbase. After a simple setup, rewards begin to appear in the account. Staking is accessible because many exchanges make it a one-click action for popular coins such as Ethereum, Cardano, or Solana.

### *How to Start Staking*

1. Pick a coin supported by staking (such as Ethereum, Cardano, Solana).
2. Set up an account on a trusted exchange (Coinbase and Kraken are good options).
3. Secure your account with strong passwords and two-factor authentication.
4. Buy or deposit your chosen coin.
5. Find the staking section and follow the steps to stake your coins.
6. Review any lockup terms—some coins allow instant withdrawal, others may have a time delay.

Staking on centralized exchanges is usually more user-friendly than using third-party wallets or validators, but the tradeoff can be higher fees or less control over advanced settings. When comparing platforms, Coinbase is known for simple interfaces and low entry requirements, while Kraken offers a wider variety of coins and detailed performance stats. Watch out for unknown platforms with limited reviews or no proof of regular audits.

### Staking Best Practices

- Always stake using a reputable, regulated exchange or a well-known decentralized wallet.
- Do not stake everything at once; start with a small amount to understand how the process works.
- Read the coin's staking lockup rules to avoid being surprised by withdrawal delays.

Now, let's look at yield farming. This strategy uses decentralized finance (DeFi) protocols to generate income by lending tokens or offering liquidity to pools. When you farm yield, you earn extra tokens or fees in exchange for making your own coins available. For example, suppose you have some USD Coin (USDC) and Ethereum (ETH). You head to a platform like Yearn Finance or PancakeSwap, connect a wallet such as MetaMask, and then deposit equal values of both coins into a liquidity pool. This pool lets others swap one token for another, and you earn a slice of the transaction fees.

## *How to Yield Farm*

1. Set up a wallet like MetaMask or Trust Wallet.
2. Transfer coins that you want to farm (for example, USDC and ETH).
3. Research pools on platforms like Yearn Finance, Uniswap, or PancakeSwap.
4. Connect your wallet to the platform.

5. Supply your tokens as instructed.
6. Monitor your earnings and learn about risks like impermanent loss.

Uniswap works well for Ethereum-based tokens with a busy trading environment. PancakeSwap focuses on the Binance Smart Chain, which may offer lower fees. Beginners should avoid platforms with high annual percentage rates but vague reputations or confusing interfaces.

### Yield Farming Best Practices

- Check if the protocol has passed third-party audits.
- Never deposit funds into contracts without clear history or transparent team backgrounds.
- Beware of coins with massive rewards that seem unsustainable over time.

The next approach is crypto lending. Here, you lend your coins through special platforms and earn interest as others borrow them. Well-known projects like Aave and Compound act as intermediaries between lenders and borrowers. If you own DAI or USDC, you deposit these stablecoins into the platform and receive regular interest payments. Getting started on Aave or Compound only takes a wallet with compatible tokens, no long applications or credit checks.

### *Steps to Start Lending*

1. Set up a wallet (MetaMask or Ledger).
2. Acquire tokens like DAI, USDC, or ETH.
3. Visit a lending platform such as Aave or Compound.

4. Connect your wallet, select "Deposit," and follow steps to lend your tokens.
5. Monitor your rate of return in real-time through the platform's dashboard.

Aave and Compound offer slightly different borrower profiles and interest calculations, but both are easy to use for new users. Watch for hidden fees, platform hacks, and any unproven new lending protocols.

### Lending Best Practices

- Stick with projects with a long track record and regular security audits.
- Keep an eye on platform health metrics to spot trouble early.
- Do not lend out coins that you cannot afford to lock up for months.

Finally, liquidity pools attract users looking to share in trading fees. When you act as a liquidity provider, you combine two kinds of tokens in a pool such as ETH and USDC on Uniswap. Each time someone swaps, you earn part of the fees generated. Alice, who has 1 ETH and 1,800 USDC, provides both to the ETH-USDC pool. After a month, she checks the pool and sees she has earned about $20 in fees, minus a slight change in her balances due to trading activity.

When choosing a pool, consider token popularity, fees, and the risk of "impermanent loss," where token values shift. Platforms like Uniswap and PancakeSwap are ideal for first-timers, with simple instructions and helpful stats.

### Liquidity Pool Best Practices

- Always research the pool's trade volume and previous returns.
- Provide liquidity with stablecoins first to minimize extreme price swings.
- Withdraw tokens promptly if the pool experiences sudden spikes or hacks.

While earning passive income in cryptocurrency opens up new possibilities, the risks and returns are always changing. To succeed, prioritize safety and risk awareness as much as potential rewards.

## Evaluating DeFi Returns, Risks, and Real Examples of Passive Earnings

Diving into DeFi income streams goes beyond just pressing a few buttons to start earning. Unlike staking a single token for a fixed reward or earning interest from a traditional savings account, returns in DeFi shift constantly. When you open a DeFi protocol and see an annual percentage yield, or APY, of 20%, that number isn't fixed in place. It can swing higher or lower by the week, day, and sometimes the hour. For someone used to a 2% fixed-interest rate from a bank or an advertised 5% staking return from a blue-chip crypto, this kind of movement might feel wild and unpredictable.

The reasons for this variability run deeper than simple market ups and downs. Every DeFi platform draws from pools of tokens provided by real users. If more liquidity floods in, yields might drop as rewards are split among extra participants. When incentives spike to attract fresh capital, maybe in the form of bonus tokens or special events, APYs can shoot up, only to drop once those events end. Protocol fees, trading activity, and even outside hype make short-term yields bounce around. This means planning for consistent passive income takes more than just picking whatever offer seems highest in the moment.

Take the example of providing liquidity in a decentralized exchange. Let's say you supply equal amounts of ETH and a stablecoin to a pool. Initially, the APY looks attractive, boosted by trading fees and token incentives. Now, picture a sudden price swing in ETH, up or down. If traders act quickly, you may end up with more of one asset and less of the other, changing the value of your holdings. This "impermanent loss" eats into the returns you were expecting, sometimes wiping out the gains from attractive APYs.

Beyond shifting yields, there's the risk tied to the code itself. A traditional bank has audited systems and government protections. In DeFi, everything runs on smart contracts, automated logic written on a blockchain. If there's a flaw, whether from sloppy programming or a clever attack, funds can disappear in minutes. Stories circulate of protocols losing millions, or all, when attackers spot a loophole. One example is a major decentralized lending platform hit by a flash loan exploit: users saw high APYs, but a bug allowed a hacker to drain the pool before anyone could react. No insurance, no reversal. Funds just gone.

Market risk also carries its own lessons. Imagine earning 50% APY from a new protocol offering shiny new tokens as rewards. If the underlying token doubles in value, your rewards grow even faster. However, the token's price crash could cancel out even high-percentage APYs if it drops by half as the hype fades. Some protocols vanish altogether in a scam, often called a "rug pull," where creators yank all the liquidity, leaving the remaining tokens worthless.

Yet for every story of sudden loss, there are practical ways investors protect their capital and sleep easier. The most reliable start with research. Check whether a platform's smart contracts have been independently audited; a public "seal of approval" means the code got at least a basic safety check. Instead of dumping every dollar into one pool, cautious users spread their holdings across several trusted protocols or asset types. This way, a single bug or market dive won't wipe out everything. Some limit their exposure to any single project, using several wallets or accounts, making tracking easier and risk lower.

Setting a rule to withdraw profits regularly locks in gains. Maybe you decide to withdraw once a week or after hitting a certain target. This buffer helps cushion against sudden dips or panic-inducing hacks. Many investors watch project news, social media, and official updates closely. If a protocol hints at changes, pauses withdrawals, or there's sudden outrage in the community, it could be a red flag to pull funds or pause adding more.

Risk-adjusted returns stay central to smart DeFi moves. Instead of getting tempted by double- or triple-digit APYs, think through what risks you're being paid to take. Higher returns usually mean absorbing bigger swings. For some, stability from large, well-known protocols trumps the dream of sky-high yields, while others experiment on a small scale with riskier projects.

Stories paint the lessons in bold. Take Lisa, who put small sums into a new DeFi farm during a market rally. She tracked APYs daily, doubled her holdings as the coins gained popularity, and harvested profits each week, building up her investment. When the bull run faded, she'd already secured a solid gain, not chasing hype but riding momentum wisely. On the other hand, Chris made a significant investment in a visually appealing new protocol. When the token crashed following a rumored hack, his significant investment disappeared almost overnight. He regrouped, read up on audits, and the next time, split his funds and stayed nimble, losing less when a project hiccuped again.

This world of DeFi passive income rewards those who stay curious, check their assumptions, and treat every protocol as a living experiment. The best results come from small, steady steps, learning as you go, always ready to adjust for what's next on the horizon.

Now that you understand the practical steps and risks involved in staking, yield farming, lending, and providing liquidity, you're better equipped to start generating passive income with cryptocurrency. Building a profitable crypto portfolio requires careful research, patience, and a willingness to learn from real-world experiences. By spreading your investments across trusted platforms and staying alert to market changes and protocol updates, you can balance potential rewards with safety. As you take these first steps, remember that steady progress and risk management will help you turn crypto opportunities into lasting wealth, setting a strong foundation for your financial future.

# CHAPTER 9
# RISK MANAGEMENT – PROTECTING YOURSELF IN A VOLATILE MARKET

More than half of all cryptocurrency investors lose money within their first year. The volatile nature of crypto markets means prices can soar one day and plummet the next, erasing months of gains in just a few hours. Many newcomers jump in, driven by excitement or fear, only to find themselves caught off guard by sudden drops, scams, or costly mistakes that drain their investments faster than they imagined. Understanding risk is not only about numbers but about knowing how to protect your assets and stay calm when markets become unpredictable. This chapter explores the importance of managing uncertainty wisely and adopting strategies that help you safeguard your investments through the constant ups and downs of crypto.

## Managing Volatility and Avoiding Common Mistakes

The world of cryptocurrency never stands still. Prices can jump or fall by 20% or more in a single day. Volatility in crypto means that values can swing wildly in ways that catch investors off guard. Just when things seem to be moving up with confidence, a sudden reversal can erase months of gains overnight. One day, Bitcoin is climbing at record speed; the next, one tweet or government regulation sends it crashing down. Ethereum has seen similar sharp drops after surges that lure newcomers in by the thousands. These gut-wrenching changes are not rare, they're expected.

A black swan event makes chaos even more unpredictable. This is the kind of sudden, rare crisis that no one sees coming, but when it strikes, it changes everything. In May 2021, a wave of negative headlines and announcements from China and Elon Musk caused a one trillion dollar wipeout across the entire crypto market within just a few days. Investors watched helplessly as coins tumbled one after another. In 2014, Mt. Gox, one of the largest Bitcoin exchanges at the time, collapsed after hackers stole hundreds of millions, leaving users with nothing. Events like these often lead to panic, confusion, and rapid losses. Managing risk begins with accepting that large, unexpected swings are part of crypto's nature. The sooner you recognize this reality, the safer your investing journey will be.

Buying crypto isn't just numbers on a screen; it brings strong feelings to the surface. Fear grabs hold after a sudden dip and pushes people to sell, locking in their losses out of panic. Greed comes out when a coin rallies, driving investors to buy more than they should as they dream of untold riches. Euphoria makes one feel invincible after a big win, tempting riskier bets that rarely end well. Panic-selling can turn a simple temporary drop into a permanent wound. Picture an investor who bought a coin at $1, watched it climb to $3, and then fall to $0.90. Driven by fear, they sell near the bottom, missing the rebound a week later, when the price returns to $2.50. Chasing pumps feels exciting until the coin dumps just as fast, leading to regret and doubt. Holding through wild swings without a plan causes stress, exhaustion, and often poor decisions. These emotional swings are natural, but unchecked, they can destroy a beginner's capital.

## *10 Most Common Mistakes Beginners Make*

1. **Investing too much in one coin**

   Putting most of your money in a single cryptocurrency can lead to big losses if that coin tanks. For example, many put everything in Luna or other hot tokens, only to see them collapse in price far quicker than expected.

2. **Following hype instead of research**

   Social media is full of "can't-lose" recommendations and viral tips. An investor might buy based on a trending hashtag, only to see the price fall as the hype fades.

3. **Ignoring stop-losses**

   Failing to use stop-loss orders means riding coins all the way down. One beginner watched their altcoin dip from $5 to $1 without protection, losing nearly their whole investment.

4. **Risking the entire portfolio**

   Going "all in" leaves no room for error. One big drop wipes out everything, while small, careful bets let you live to try again.

5. **Forgetting security practices**

   Using weak passwords or leaving coins on exchanges puts investments at risk of hacks or scams. One investor found their balance gone overnight after leaving funds on a shady platform.

6. **Ignoring transaction fees**

High fees on trades and transfers eat into profits, shrinking gains and turning a winning trade into a losing one.

7. **Falling for herd mentality**

Following the crowd into "the next big thing" can backfire. Many rushed into Dogecoin at its peak then panicked as prices crashed, following the next herd elsewhere.

8. **Overleveraging**

Trading with borrowed funds when new to crypto can multiply losses quickly. Some see liquidations erase their capital in a flash.

9. **Neglecting to take profits**

Holding forever in hopes of higher gains, some investors watch strong positions fade back to their entry point or worse.

10. **Trusting scams and quick-rich schemes**

Scams promising triple returns lure beginners. One example: an investor bought into a "guaranteed 10x" project announced on Telegram, only to lose all their funds when the creators vanished.

### *Risk Management Strategies*

Diversifying across different coins and sectors reduces the risk of a single failure ending your progress. For instance, a balanced portfolio might hold 60 percent in Bitcoin and Ethereum, 20 percent in established altcoins, and 20 percent in cash or stablecoins. Setting clear risk limits helps protect you; never invest more than you are comfortable losing. Position sizing ensures that no single trade can threaten your entire account. Stop-loss orders can automatically limit losses when prices move against you. Every purchase should follow a risk-versus-reward mindset, where you carefully weigh potential losses against possible gains before buying. Sticking to these habits, even on turbulent days, keeps your footing steady. When unexpected events strike, such as flash crashes or hacks, you respond with your plan instead of reacting in panic.

Becoming aware of risk and learning how to manage it puts you ahead of most new investors. Understanding common pitfalls and keeping emotions under control gives you the tools to stay balanced and confident. This mindset helps you think long term and face challenges and scams with clarity. Staying alert and practicing consistent caution allows you to protect what you build while continuing to explore new opportunities.

## Identifying Scams and Building Investor Resilience

After experiencing the sharp ups and downs of crypto prices, every investor feels their emotions pulling them in risky directions. Markets rise and fall in dramatic swings, tempting many to act on excitement, fear, or blind hope that luck alone will protect their money. The truth is that volatile conditions are exactly what scammers and fraudsters rely on. When emotions run high, it becomes harder to pause, think clearly, and spot warning signs before sending funds or acting on suspicious opportunities. That's when costly mistakes happen.

Criminals use increasingly clever tactics to exploit investor trust. Phishing scams, for example, involve fake websites or emails designed to trick you into revealing your login details or private keys. These often look almost identical to legitimate crypto sites or exchanges. Rug pulls occur when a project team launches a new cryptocurrency or decentralized finance token, builds excitement, collects investor funds, and then disappears, leaving behind worthless coins. Ponzi schemes lure people with promises of high, steady returns but pay early investors with money from new ones. Once the flow of fresh cash stops, the scheme collapses, and most participants lose everything. Fake giveaways are another common trap on social media, where accounts claim they can double your coins if you send some first, but nothing ever comes back.

Spotting these tricks starts with paying attention to details. Be wary of vague or missing information about who is behind a coin or platform. Anonymous teams often avoid accountability. Promises of guaranteed profits or fast riches break the basic rules of real investing. If it sounds too good to be true, it almost always is. Sudden social media hype with little substance, especially when many influencers promote the same project at once, is another major warning sign. Projects without clear whitepapers, working products, or open community discussions are red flags. Legitimate ventures usually share open-source code and undergo independent audits to prove transparency, while scams often skip these entirely.

To check whether a project is genuine, start by reading its whitepaper carefully. Look for clear explanations, achievable goals, and a realistic timeline. Research the team's background using professional profiles or past work in blockchain development. Community discussions on Reddit or established crypto forums can reveal important concerns that official channels may hide. A few hours of due diligence can save you from losses that take months or even years to recover. Check if the project or its smart contracts have been reviewed by recognized security auditors. Before putting any money in, see if news about the project comes from trusted sources, not just anonymous Twitter threads or Telegram groups.

Keeping your crypto safe day to day requires a few consistent habits. Always use established exchanges and wallets with a proven reputation. Double-check website URLs before logging in, since phishing attacks often use addresses that look almost identical to real ones but differ by a single letter. Enable two-factor authentication on every account to make hacking far more difficult. Never share your private key, seed phrase, or wallet backup with anyone, no matter what they promise or offer.

Cases like the Squid Game token rug pull show exactly what can go wrong. The token's creators rode a wave of hype, built a website and a Twitter presence, then vanished with millions after the price spiked, leaving buyers with nothing. A bit of deeper research would have quickly shown that none of the original show's creators or Netflix had any involvement or approval. No audit, no transparent team, and no verified partnership were all clear signs to walk away.

Short-term thinking often fuels the success of scammers. Chasing viral coins or quick returns might look smart at first, but it usually ends in sudden crashes or scams that erase profits overnight. Real stories repeat the same lesson. One trader jumped into ten meme coins during a bull run and briefly saw massive paper profits, only to lose nearly everything when nine of them collapsed. Meanwhile, investors who focused on solid projects, practiced dollar-cost averaging, held diversified portfolios, and avoided hype grew their wealth gradually but consistently over time.

Steady investing is safer and builds both confidence and resilience. Mistakes are part of every investor's path. The most successful crypto investors are not the ones who never lose, but the ones who learn, adapt, and recover smarter after setbacks. Keep a record of every investment, including the reason behind each decision, and revisit your goals regularly. Reacting emotionally to every price movement leads to regret, but responding with patience and a plan pays off. Engage with other thoughtful investors, share experiences, and learn from both your wins and your missteps.

Staying vigilant protects your assets, but each choice builds trust in your own process. Keep learning, refining your approach, and surrounding yourself with reliable information and level-headed voices. This is how lasting confidence grows and how you stay one step ahead of the next wave of market hype and deception.

Now that you understand the risks and common pitfalls in crypto investing, you can approach the market with a clear plan and steady mindset. By managing volatility through smart strategies like diversification, risk limits, and stop-losses, you protect your investments from sudden shocks and emotional decisions. Staying vigilant against scams and hype means you keep your hard-earned money safe and focused on legitimate opportunities. With these tools in hand, you're ready to build a balanced portfolio that aligns with your goals, navigate unpredictable markets confidently, and grow your crypto wealth over time.

# CHAPTER 10
# CRYPTO TAXES AND LEGAL CONSIDERATIONS

Have you ever paused mid-transaction, wondering how the government views that trade or sale of your cryptocurrency? Or perhaps you've asked yourself if it matters to keep a record every time you swap one token for another, even when the amounts seem small. If these questions have crossed your mind, you're not alone. The world of crypto taxes and legal rules can feel like a maze, where every move might trigger hidden obligations and unexpected paperwork.

This chapter steps into that complex landscape, bringing clarity to what really counts, why recordkeeping matters, and how staying organized keeps you in control. Understanding the full picture is not only about following the rules but also about protecting yourself and your profits. Knowing how to manage taxes and legal responsibilities turns confusion into confidence, helping you navigate your crypto journey with precision and peace of mind, no matter your experience level.

## Understanding Crypto Taxation and Tracking Transactions

### *Understanding How Countries Tax Crypto*

People across the world ask the same question: How does my government tax cryptocurrency? No matter where you live, the answer almost always starts the same way. Most countries, including the United States, the European Union, the United Kingdom, Canada, and Australia, treat cryptocurrencies as property or assets rather than actual money. This distinction has major consequences for how trading, storing, and spending are taxed.

In the United States, every time you sell crypto, trade it for another coin, or use it to buy goods or services, you trigger what's called a taxable event. The IRS requires you to pay capital gains tax on any profit you earn. If you mine, stake, or otherwise earn cryptocurrency, that counts as income and comes with its own set of rules. Simply buying and holding coins without selling does not create any tax obligation until you eventually sell or exchange them.

Things aren't much different in the European Union or United Kingdom. There, selling, swapping, earning, and spending crypto are all reportable. Canada follows a similar approach: the sale, trade, or even conversion between coins is a taxable event. Australia taxes most crypto activity through capital gains tax, so even exchanging one token for another is something the authorities want to know about.

Readers often wonder: Will the government notice a small purchase or casual trade? The fact is, even trades between tokens, or spending your coins on something small, should be tracked. A scenario might help: You buy Bitcoin, then use some to purchase a cup of coffee, and a week later send some to a friend in another country. Each activity might trigger income or capital gains tax, depending on the jurisdiction. From a tax perspective, every time crypto changes hands, so does your tax obligation.

### *What Makes Crypto Tracking Tricky*

Investing in traditional stocks or real estate is usually straightforward. You buy shares in a brokerage account, collect dividends, and sell later. Everything stays in one account with clean records. Crypto doesn't work that way.

The speed and variety of crypto transactions mean a single investor might juggle dozens or even hundreds of trades per year. Prices change minute to minute, so the "cost basis" - the price you paid for something that determines your gains or losses - is constantly shifting. When you add transfers between exchanges and wallets, it becomes very easy to lose track.

Consider a typical hobbyist trader. They buy Ethereum on one exchange, then transfer it to a private wallet. From there, they might swap part of it for Solana using a decentralized exchange. Later, they purchase a digital artwork (NFT) with some leftover ETH. Each move happens at different prices, times, and fee structures. Every action affects what you owe at tax time, so keeping accurate and organized records is essential to staying compliant.

### *Steps for Tracking Trades, Gains, and Losses*

Good recordkeeping is not optional. Track every crypto move with care, even if the numbers seem small. Here's a structured approach that keeps things organized:

- List transaction dates, from purchases to trades to sales
- Record the exact amount and name of the coin or token
- Capture buy/sell prices at the transaction moment, in your local currency
- Save records of network, trading, or exchange fees, you often get to subtract these from your gains
- Note the type of transaction: was it a buy, sell, trade, stake reward, or gift?
- Maintain documentation, like receipts, transaction IDs, and screenshots when possible

Even minor actions, like sending coins to a new wallet or swapping a small amount, add up over a year. Missing even a single transaction can snowball into trouble during an audit. Accuracy is the best defense.

### *Software That Makes Life Easier*

Manual record-keeping quickly becomes overwhelming. Crypto tax software tools like CoinTracker, Koinly, and TaxBit can help. These services connect directly to most popular exchanges and wallets.

- Import all your transaction data instantly from your exchange accounts
- Sync wallet transactions, including deposits and withdrawals

- Review auto-generated tax reports, including calculations for gains, losses, and cost basis
- Find flagged issues, like missing or duplicated transactions

Always check the automatic reports for errors or missing information before filing. The more sources you have, the more likely you'll spot duplicate records or overlooked fees.

### *An Example That Covers Every Scenario*

Consider a reader who buys $1,000 worth of Bitcoin on Coinbase. Step one: record the date, amount, and fees. They transfer $500 in BTC to a private wallet. This action is not taxable, but it still needs to be tracked for accurate recordkeeping. Next, they trade $300 worth of BTC for Ethereum on a decentralized exchange. That trade is a taxable event, so they should note the value on the trading day and the price of the ETH received. Finally, they sell the ETH on another exchange for dollars. That sale is also a taxable event, and all details should be logged. Each swap or sale requires updating your records with the latest figures.

Staying organized and informed keeps your investments safe and compliant, building a strong habit that will serve you well throughout your crypto journey.

## Compliance, Audit Preparation, and Record-Keeping Best Practices

As you actively track every gain, loss, and transaction in your crypto portfolio, there's another level of safety you need for full protection: preparation for an audit or sudden regulatory review.

Just as tax frameworks and tracking tools give structure to your trading history, audit readiness goes a step further by demanding meticulous records and clear explanations for every movement of funds. Audits can be triggered by a range of scenarios, anything from a misreported decimal point to discrepancies between your filings and records collected by exchanges or third parties to completely random selection. Tax authorities are increasingly matching wallet activity and exchange data against declared income. They can request access to every transaction that might shift your balance, including incoming transfers, outgoing payments, staking rewards, and even seemingly minor conversions between stablecoins.

It helps to stay ready with an audit file for each year. You should be prepared to provide information such as

- Complete lists of wallet and exchange addresses you control (both hot and cold storage)
- Detailed transaction logs from exchanges and wallets (CSV or spreadsheet format)
- Screenshots or PDF statements showing trade histories and balances
- Records of wallet-to-wallet transfers, including explanations for each transfer
- Supporting documentation for staking, lending, or DeFi activities
- A log of fiat on-ramps or off-ramps, showing bank deposits or withdrawals connected to crypto transactions

Regularly updating this file means you won't scramble to track down fragments of information years later. If an auditor requests clarification, you can quickly supply any document or screenshot to prove your case. Imagine facing an inquiry about a major swap made three years prior. If all it takes is opening your digital folder, finding the transaction hash, attached explanation, and a PDF from the relevant exchange, you save time and reduce stress. Missing or incomplete records only increase audit duration and the risk of penalties.

Rules around crypto taxation evolve as governments adapt to new forms of trading and investment. Each year might bring changes: mandatory reporting of wallet holdings, stricter reporting on offshore exchanges, or requirements to declare NFT transactions. Ignoring these shifts puts your compliance at risk. Subscribing to reliable sources keeps you ahead. Watch for updates published by national tax authorities, such as the IRS, HMRC, or the ATO, or alerts from reputable tax platforms and certified advisors. Consider setting a calendar reminder for a yearly portfolio review so you routinely double-check for changes affecting crypto reporting.

Keeping up with these changes means using tools that incorporate new requirements. Many leading tax software providers update their systems after every policy shift, allowing you to adapt quickly. But never assume automation covers every detail. Manual checklists help. Review the following annually:

- Are all exchanges and wallets accounted for?
- Have new asset types (like NFTs or DeFi tokens) been included in records?
- Are all deposit and withdrawal records accessible and backed up?
- Is each transaction annotated with its business purpose and context?
- Has the software or template you use incorporated recent legal changes?

Maintaining pristine records starts with a simple, workable system. Begin with a master spreadsheet listing every transaction by date, type, asset, amount, source, and destination. For added security, download and store all monthly account statements from every exchange or wallet. These should be saved in both a secure cloud folder and an offline storage device, ideally with encrypted backups. Alongside your automated tracking, keep a folder of "manual notes", text files, or PDFs describing the reason for transfers, staking arrangements, or asset swaps.

Annotating transactions clarifies intent. If you move ETH from Exchange A to a private wallet, record in your log, "Transfer for cold storage, no sale occurred." For a staking reward, attach a brief note describing the protocol and the approximate APY at the time. This habit eliminates guesswork during future tax returns or audits. Spreadsheets act as a safety net if automated tools miss or misclassify a transaction.

Practically, thorough record-keeping transforms tax preparation. Investors who keep annotated records, digital receipts, and backup logs can generate annual tax reports within hours instead of days. In several cases, an investor faced with an audit provided a zip file containing all documents, transaction hashes, and explanations enabling a short, low-stress audit rather than a protracted investigation.

Compliance brings more than audit survival. Only rock-solid records protect against suspicion and fines as regulations change and authorities use blockchain analytics to trace funds across networks. Though crypto might appear anonymous, that's a fading myth, wallet addresses are now mapped, and exchanges report activity as standard practice. Confidence comes from knowing you can answer any question about your portfolio, no matter who's asking.

This peace of mind lets you focus on long-term growth, knowing that your foundation is solid. You'll face law changes, or that unwelcome letter from the tax authority, not with panic, but with the certainty that your preparation puts you firmly in control of your financial future.

Now that you understand how cryptocurrency is taxed and why careful tracking and record-keeping are essential, you're equipped to navigate this complex landscape with confidence. By staying organized, using the right tools, and keeping up with changing rules, you can protect yourself from costly mistakes and audits while maximizing your investment potential. This solid foundation allows you to focus on growing your crypto portfolio strategically and legally, turning your ambitions into real financial progress without the stress of uncertainty.

CHAPTER 11

# THE FUTURE OF CRYPTO – WEB3, AI, AND BEYOND

"Why should I trust a computer program with my money when banks have always handled it?" That question echoes in the minds of many who hear about crypto and blockchain for the first time. It's a fair concern; after all, handing over control to technology rather than familiar institutions feels risky and confusing. But what if that very shift could unlock new opportunities for managing your finances, proving your identity, or even owning pieces of things you never thought possible? As technologies like blockchain and artificial intelligence evolve, they're quietly reshaping how we interact with money and information. These aren't just abstract ideas for experts; they're tools that anyone eager to learn can use to take more control over their financial future. Understanding the true value behind each innovation without succumbing to hype is crucial for navigating this new landscape. This chapter invites you to step beyond skepticism and explore how these emerging technologies might fit into your journey toward smarter investing and greater financial freedom.

## Technological Shifts: Blockchain, AI, and Emerging Trends

Few changes promise as much for personal finance and opportunity as blockchain. At its core, blockchain is a record-keeping system that works without a central authority, letting users interact, earn, lend, and invest on new terms. The shift to decentralized finance, or DeFi, is already unlocking possibilities that mainstream banks can't match. Imagine lending money on a platform that connects you directly with borrowers without needing a bank's approval. These peer-to-peer platforms let people set their own rates, sometimes in countries where opening a bank account is hard or where traditional loans cost too much to make sense. Sending money home from abroad follows similar rules. Blockchains allow remittances across borders for a tiny fraction of what money-transfer services charge. For millions of families, that small difference in cost means more money where it's needed.

Beyond moving cash, blockchain is also changing the way we prove and manage who we are. Right now, personal details like driver's licenses, school records, work credentials, sit in government or company silos. If you lose a password or paperwork, that can mean headaches or lost chances. A digital identity built on blockchain puts individuals in control instead. Credentials live in a crypto wallet you manage, protected by encryption. For example, think about a freelancer wanting to show proof of skills to a potential client. Using a blockchain-based resume, they can securely share only the pieces needed, with no central authority in the way. This approach makes moving between jobs, countries, or online platforms safer and faster.

Ownership, too, looks different on blockchains. Tokenization turns assets into digital tokens that represent real-world value, opening up ownership to a wider pool of investors. Small investors can now own fractions instead of needing thousands to buy a slice of a start-up or a chunk of real estate. Non-fungible tokens, or NFTs, draw the most buzz. Digital art is just the start. Items like rare collectibles, event tickets, or shares in a classic car can all be managed and traded on-chain. These changes aren't just for tech enthusiasts; they give everyone a shot at new types of value.

Crypto's next promise is merging with artificial intelligence. One way this happens is with AI-powered trading bots. Normally, managing a set of crypto investments takes time and skill. Some projects let users tap into pre-built bots that analyze market data, automate trades, and even shift strategies on their own. In another trend, blockchains are being used to verify where the data that feeds AI models comes from. Since AI models rely on giant sets of information, trust is everything. A blockchain trail makes it easier to spot tampering and protect against misinformation, which is helpful for things like medical research or legal analysis.

That said, not every new combo of crypto and AI works out as promised. Some companies claim "intelligent blockchains" that make decisions on their own, but in reality, these systems often struggle outside controlled settings. A well-known project in 2023 offered AI-based security on the blockchain, boasting instant scam detection. Early users found that, while some fraud was caught, the system missed subtler tricks and had trouble adapting to new threats. While AI tools in crypto can automate tasks and reduce manual labor, human oversight is still necessary. A trading algorithm might boost profit on good days but crash in a volatile market. Investors who trust these systems without understanding the risks sometimes end up disappointed.

Maintaining composure and a steady checklist is crucial when navigating the constantly changing crypto world. The strongest projects rest on sound code, regular audits, and open communities. Useful crypto products solve real problems like lowering transfer costs or helping manage identity. Look for signs of real adoption: are people using the platform, and do experienced developers back it up? Regulatory trends matter as well. If a project dodges questions about compliance, that's a warning sign.

Red flags stand out with a little practice. Vague whitepapers that dodge technical details, big promises backed only by a famous face, or tokens with no clear use case often signal more hype than value. A solid investment asks for careful thought, not just excitement.

Curiosity leads the way, but mixing skepticism with excitement helps avoid costly mistakes. As the ground shifts under your feet, staying open while vetting each chance on its facts, not just feelings, offers the best shot for safe progress. Every new feature or product can hint at where the future is heading, and the sharpest paths combine learning, patience, and self-protection as these opportunities take shape.

## Practical Implications: Your Role, Opportunities, and Sensible Strategies

As crypto and AI merge further into daily life, they create tools and opportunities for everyone, not just early tech adopters. Blockchains automate and record financial and legal activities. AI sorts data, finds patterns, and helps people make decisions.

Combining these forces means regular people will soon handle their money, work, and digital identity in new ways. For investors, freelancers, or employees, learning to use these tools will be as basic as learning to use a smartphone is today.

Picture yourself investing using decentralized finance (DeFi) platforms instead of a traditional bank. You might deposit coins into a decentralized savings protocol that pays higher interest for holding your assets. Unlike a regular bank account, your funds are spread across a smart contract code that runs itself based on set rules making transactions fast and transparent. When you need a loan or want to trade, you interact directly with the platform, skipping paperwork and extra fees. No need to trust a single company; instead, you trust the code and the network.

For creatives, non-fungible tokens (NFTs) give a path to new income. An author, musician, or designer can release a limited-edition digital product as an NFT. Each token proves authenticity and ownership, so fans can resell or trade digital collectibles the same way rare comic books or vinyl records once were. A small royalty fee goes back to the creator each time an NFT changes hands, making creative work more profitable and sustainable. This same technology may extend to intellectual property like patents for inventors or thesis papers for scholars giving anyone an easy and trackable way to license or share their work.

Small business owners and freelancers could join decentralized autonomous organizations (DAOs). These groups, run fully by code and community votes, pool resources for business ventures, investments, or passion projects. As a member, you might help vote on where funds go or submit your ideas for the group to back. The process is open, and all decisions are stored on a blockchain for everyone to see. As more companies experiment with DAOs, professionals will need to understand these governance models and the digital wallets used to participate.

Another change comes in the form of blockchain-verified identity. Instead of relying on a stack of paper documents or passwords, you hold a digital credential in your crypto wallet, a record that only you control, proving your skills, work history, or education. Employers or clients can instantly check these badges, speeding up hiring, making remote work easier, and letting gig workers collect references from anywhere in the world. This shifts the traditional resume and job-seeking process to a globally trusted, secure, and instantly accessible format.

Stepping back, the question becomes: how do you spot the next opportunity without taking on too much risk? Success in crypto rarely comes from chasing every trend. Instead, set clear rules to evaluate what is worth your time and money. Here's a simple framework:

1. **Real-world use:** Does the project solve a real problem or make something easier for people or businesses?
2. **Team transparency:** Who is building the project? Can you find their names, past work, and public commitments?
3. **Technology credibility:** Has the technology been tested? Are there audits, code reviews, or partnerships with reliable companies?
4. **Community support:** Is there active discussion on forums, social media, or developer chats? Do real users contribute and point out flaws or suggest improvements?
5. **Roadmap and whitepaper:** Does the project have a clear plan? Can you understand what they want to build and why?

Before investing, read the whitepaper closely. Look for clear writing, honest discussion of risks, and simple diagrams of how the system works. Caution if you notice grand promises but no details. Check the leadership; can you verify their past success? Search for recent updates and if promises are being met. For example, many early investors in Ethereum saw progress on long-term milestones and engagement from a skilled team. By contrast, meme coins, or short-lived hype tokens, often lacked serious documentation, leadership, or genuine community support, and many disappeared as fast as they grew.

To stay ahead but avoid hype fatigue, create a personal strategy. Only track two or three projects and document why you chose them and your exit or review plan. Split your portfolio with strict rules, capping how much you risk on any one idea. Write down your reasons for every decision and revisit them monthly, not daily. Reliable success builds on patience, skepticism, and a willingness to learn as the tech changes.

Make ongoing learning a habit. Follow developer blogs from trusted people. Listen to select podcasts known for balanced insight, not hype. Join one or two online groups where people challenge bad ideas and engage in open discussion. If you want to go further, look for short, focused courses on concepts you don't understand yet.

Most of all, remember that adapting to the crypto future is about steady effort, not wild bets. Be curious, but demand evidence before acting. Grow your skills reading contract code, understanding wallet basics, and using simple DeFi tools so you're prepared to judge each new wave of change as it arrives. Holding onto these habits gives you the best chance to benefit, no matter where crypto and AI lead next.

Now that we understand how blockchain and AI are reshaping finance, identity, and ownership, the path forward is clear: success comes from blending curiosity with careful judgment. These technologies open doors to new ways of investing, working, and creating value if you approach them with patience, learn steadily, and rely on real evidence over hype. By focusing on projects that solve genuine problems, backed by transparent teams and active communities, you position yourself to navigate this evolving landscape wisely. With a solid strategy and ongoing education, you can turn emerging crypto opportunities into lasting financial growth, making smart choices today that build your wealth tomorrow.

CHAPTER 12

# YOUR ACTION PLAN – FROM BEGINNER TO INVESTOR

Nearly half of all new investors quit within their first year, not because they lack funds but because they struggle to turn plans into action. It's easy to get stuck reading about strategies or waiting for the perfect moment to start. Yet investing isn't a spectator sport; it requires setting clear goals, making choices, and learning through experience.

Taking that first step can feel daunting, as uncertainty, risk, and complex language create barriers that keep many people on the sidelines. But confidence doesn't come from theory alone; it grows through doing. This chapter focuses on crossing that line from hesitation to hands-on investing, helping beginners build a foundation rooted in purpose and clarity. By taking practical actions such as defining what you want, choosing investments that match your comfort level, and tracking your progress, you begin to shape your own story as an investor, one decision at a time.

## Laying the Groundwork: Planning Your First Steps in Investing

Setting clear and realistic investing goals shapes every decision you make next. Picture what success means for you. Some want to build long-term wealth to beat inflation. Others hope to earn extra monthly income. Begin with a personal statement written for your eyes only honest and specific. Try something like, “I want to see my initial $1,000 grow over three years so I can plan a future trip,” or “I want to learn how to generate income through staking rewards and see my crypto savings grow by 6% each year.” A clear reason builds focus, and that focus keeps you on track when markets are noisy.

Personal finance always comes with risk. Crypto investing involves more ups and downs than a savings account, so it’s important to think seriously about your comfort with risk. Take a minute to jot down some honest answers:

- Are you okay seeing the value of your investments change by 10–20% or more in a short time?
- How would you feel if you logged in and saw your portfolio drop in value for a few weeks in a row?
- Are these funds set aside for long-term goals, or would you need them soon for emergencies?
- Will losing your investment make you lose sleep—or can you treat it as a lesson?

Matching your investing goals and comfort with risk lays the foundation for every smart decision that follows. If dramatic price swings make you anxious, focus on a slow and steady path toward growth. If you are more comfortable with uncertainty, you can take on a little more risk, but always within clear limits.

Once you understand your motivation, turn your attention to selecting your first cryptocurrencies and a reliable platform. For most beginners, ease of use, security, and access to major coins matter most. Bitcoin and Ethereum are excellent starting points. Both have stood the test of time, with large global communities and proven stability. If you want variety, consider adding a third coin such as Solana or Cardano, but stay away from tokens that promise instant wealth or appear only because of online trends.

Next, choose a trustworthy exchange. A crypto exchange is a platform where you can buy, sell, or trade digital currencies. Look for one that offers a simple sign-up process and strong security. Well-known choices for new investors include Coinbase, Kraken, and Binance US. Before you register, review their password protection policies, confirm that they support two-factor authentication, and compare fees. High transaction costs can quietly eat into your gains. Avoid smaller or lesser-known exchanges, especially those with flashy marketing, unclear information, or reports of frozen withdrawals.

Finally, consider how you will store your crypto. Some exchanges hold coins on your behalf, which is convenient at first, but storing them in your own wallet gives you more control and long-term security. For beginners, using the exchange's built-in wallet is fine. As you gain confidence, learn how to transfer your assets to a private app called a non-custodial wallet. Choose one with an easy recovery process, strong reviews, and reliable customer support.

Building your starter portfolio means choosing just two or three coins and spreading your money between them. Here's an example for someone investing $1,000:

- $600 in Bitcoin (BTC)
- $300 in Ethereum (ETH)
- $100 in Solana (SOL) or Cardano (ADA)

Start small, only invest what you're willing to lose, and treat every dollar as a tool for learning. Avoid over-diversifying; too many coins make tracking and research a headache. A focused approach gives you a front-row seat to the basics, from price moves to real-world news affecting your holdings.

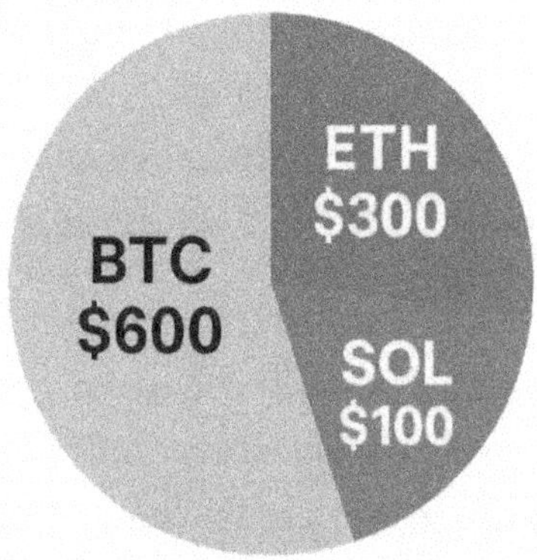


Now you need a tracking system. The habit of recording buys, sells, and balances keeps you engaged and prevents emotional reactions. For many, a simple spreadsheet works best. Columns for date, coin, amount, price paid, and current value show clearly what you own. Some prefer a free tracker app made for crypto, which often links directly to exchanges and updates in real time. Or use a notebook; consistency matters more than the tool. On payday or at a set point each month, review and add notes on any important events or price swings. A log helps you make sense of the journey and adds clarity every time you check in.

Getting started with goal setting, coin selection, and tracking habits puts you in control. Every recorded decision builds confidence, turning theory into clear action. This foundation gives you the experience to move forward, and your first portfolio becomes more than a collection of coins; it's your training ground, ready to teach you with every step you take. The next section guides you through growing this starter approach into real-world learning, so you build up both skills and wealth as you go.

## Taking Action: Building Confidence Through Practical Experience

Every successful crypto investor remembers their first steps: the nerves, the uncertainty, maybe even a bit of excitement as they placed a tiny buy order or explored a new wallet. That sense of moving from theory to practice unlocks real growth. Having set your broad goals and carefully built your first portfolio, you now get to build on your courage and organization by learning directly through hands-on action. The most valuable teacher in the crypto world is experience; each mini-experiment builds confidence in ways that planning alone can't. Even small steps are solid progress, letting you see for yourself how markets, platforms, and currencies behave in real time.

Imagine someone buying $50 worth of Ethereum for the very first time. They choose a well-known, widely supported coin, compare a few apps to find one that feels straightforward, and set up a secure wallet before pressing "Buy." Almost immediately, they notice that confirmation times vary and that transaction fees can reduce the total. A few minutes later, seeing ETH appear in their wallet feels like crossing a threshold from spectator to genuine investor. They jot down notes about what went smoothly, what was confusing, and what surprised them. That first trade becomes the foundation for the next step: maybe researching why fees change throughout the day or testing another exchange with a small amount. Bit by bit, these small actions build understanding that lasts.

Active investing does not require large sums of money or advanced technical knowledge. Most beginners find that confidence grows each time they take a manageable risk and review the outcome with curiosity and patience. For example, someone might set aside $25 worth of a token to experiment with staking, not to chase high rewards but to learn how platforms pay earnings and process withdrawals. By checking their staking dashboard weekly, tracking rewards, and noting any issues or delays, they gain insights that reading alone could never provide.

You can turn these small experiments into steady habits with a few simple tools. A compact notebook, digital or paper, works perfectly as an investing journal. After each trade or new experience, take a moment to answer a few short prompts that help you reflect on what you learned, what worked, and what to adjust next:

- What worked that I might use again?
- What was more complicated than I expected?
- What new question do I have after seeing the results?
- What would I try next time to improve the result?

Spread these reflections out in bullet points or a quick table if that feels easier. The trick is to capture your own thinking while the memory is fresh, making it easy to spot patterns and build reliable routines over time. Spreadsheets help too: track the dates of trades, platforms used, fees paid, and changes in portfolio size. You'll soon see that every entry is a clue for better decisions down the road.

To keep decisions steady and avoid being rattled by impulsive news alerts, try using a "pause and verify" checklist before each move. Have you double-checked wallet addresses? Have you skimmed recent news or social media about the project? Are fees within your expected range? If anything feels off or confusing, stop and review. This quick, repeatable habit turns what used to be scary into a straightforward part of your investing plan.

Here's how you can put learning-by-doing into practice:

First, recognize that small, live experiments teach you what books and videos can't. Handling even a modest trade lets you feel how platforms work, see real numbers change, and get the emotional experience of gaining, or losing, a dollar or two in value. These lessons last because you lived them, not just studied them.

Try this step-by-step activity:

1. Pick a well-known coin such as BTC or ETH.
2. Buy a small amount (as little as $10 if the app allows it).
3. Record in your tracker or notebook everything you notice about the process; timing, fees, ease of use.
4. Watch how your portfolio number moves for a few days.

5. Answer reflection questions:

- How did the transaction compare to what I expected?
- What did I learn from seeing real price changes?
- Would I do anything differently on my next trade?

6. Challenge yourself to repeat with a new coin, a different exchange, or a feature like staking or swapping, recording each new insight.

Throughout this book, you will keep building on these action-based skills. Each new topic and strategy connects to practical investing steps, allowing your experience to grow alongside your portfolio and knowledge. Testing ideas, reflecting honestly, and recording what you learn takes fear out of the process and helps you create your own guide for staying safe, adapting to changing markets, and developing as an investor. Every action, whether successful or not, lays the groundwork for smarter decisions and stronger confidence each time you step into the crypto world.

Now that you have built a solid foundation by setting clear goals, choosing your first coins, and establishing habits to track and reflect on your progress, you are ready to move forward with confidence from planning into active learning through real-world experience. Each small trade and every note you take sharpens your understanding and builds resilience against the ups and downs of crypto markets. By embracing this hands-on approach, you turn theory into practical knowledge that grows alongside your portfolio. As you continue on this journey, these early steps will prepare you to explore new strategies, manage risks wisely, and steadily build the skills and confidence needed to make your crypto investments work for your financial future.

# BE THE VOICE THAT INSPIRES FINANCIAL FREEDOM

One of life's greatest truths is that when we share what we have learned, we empower others to grow. Every insight we pass on can light the way for someone just beginning their journey.

Think for a moment about how you felt when you first considered investing in cryptocurrency. Were you excited by the possibilities? Are you uncertain about the risks involved? Are you curious but hesitant to take the first step?

Now picture another reader standing in that same place. They are hearing about Bitcoin, Ethereum, altcoins, NFTs, and blockchain, but they are not sure where to start or how to invest wisely without losing confidence.

This is where your review can make a real difference. By sharing your honest reflections, you help others decide whether this guide offers the strategies, clarity, and encouragement they need to move forward.

Your words can inspire confidence and remind others that financial freedom begins with knowledge, discipline, and courage. Thank you for being part of this journey. Your voice matters, and by leaving a review, you are helping make cryptocurrency investing more accessible for every reader who follows in your footsteps.

# CONCLUSION

As you reach this final page, take a moment to reflect on how far you have come. If you began this journey uncertain about crypto, unsure of what it really is or how everyday people actually profit from it, you are not alone. Crypto investing can seem mysterious and intimidating, full of technical jargon, wild price swings, and headlines that make it sound either like a perfect get-rich-quick scheme or an elaborate scam. But now you hold something most newcomers never achieve: a clear understanding of what the world of digital assets truly offers, and practical strategies for building lasting wealth.

You have learned that success in crypto does not require genius-level tech skills. It requires curiosity, common sense, a solid plan, and the commitment to treat your financial future as something worth learning for. Throughout these pages, you have discovered that crypto's potential for wealth-building is not reserved for computer scientists or Silicon Valley insiders. It belongs to anyone who prepares, studies, and approaches investing with discipline and patience.

Crypto rewards those who are ready and patient. One of the biggest mistakes new investors make is believing they must act quickly—jumping on trends, chasing the hottest coins, or trying to time the market. You now know the truth: the investors who succeed, whether by holding strong assets like Bitcoin and Ethereum or by exploring new opportunities such as NFTs and DeFi, are the ones who do their homework first. They research before investing, create a clear risk management plan, and balance their portfolios based on long-term goals rather than online noise.

Let's face it, there will always be hype in crypto. There will always be people promising quick riches or the next big "moonshot." But as you have seen, there are smarter ways to build and sustain real wealth. You do not need to abandon common sense or rush in blindly. Your power lies in your ability to understand the rules, recognize opportunities, and stay calm when others lose control. You already hold one of the greatest advantages in this space: you know you do not know everything, and you are willing to keep learning.

That humility and curiosity set you apart. Too many investors believe they must predict every move or understand blockchain technology in full detail. The truth is simpler: you only need a thoughtful plan that fits your personal financial goals and comfort with risk. Whether your aim is long-term growth, passive income, or diversification beyond traditional assets, your journey begins with a few key steps that anyone can take. No coding skills or full-time trading are required.

So what comes next? The answer is simple: action. Over the next 90 days, you have a real opportunity to take control, move forward, and start building your own foundation for digital wealth.

Here are practical steps to put what you have learned into motion:

**Review your finances honestly.** Decide what portion of your income or savings you can safely allocate to crypto. Remember, starting small is not just a saying; it is how nearly every successful investor begins. Even a modest investment allows you to gain experience without risking more than you can afford to lose.

**Secure your accounts.** Open accounts only with reputable exchanges and wallets. Turn on two-factor authentication, back up your private keys, and double-check where sensitive information is stored. In crypto, protecting your capital is not only wise but essential.

**Choose your first assets carefully.** Apply what you have learned about the different types of cryptocurrencies, from established coins like Bitcoin and Ethereum to promising altcoins or tokens with genuine utility. Ask yourself: What problem does this project solve? Who is behind it? What makes it stand out? The best investments rarely come from hype; they come from understanding and insight.

**Build your portfolio slowly, keeping diversity and balance in mind.** Allocate your funds across different categories such as blue-chip coins, promising smaller projects, and perhaps a small portion in innovative areas like NFTs or DeFi if you feel ready. Rebalance your portfolio periodically, just as you would with traditional investments.

**Keep managing your risks**. Set stop-loss orders if you trade, and never invest money you will need in the short term. Use dollar-cost averaging instead of trying to time every high and low. Above all, separate your emotions from daily price movements.

The market will swing wildly, but your goal is to stay consistent with your plan.

**Explore multiple income strategies at your own pace.** You may want to try staking, lending, or earning passive yield through decentralized finance platforms. Start small and research thoroughly before committing. Each tool carries its own risks but also offers the potential for strong returns when used wisely.

**Continue your education.** The blockchain world evolves quickly, so staying informed is essential. Choose trusted sources such as newsletters, podcasts, and YouTube channels that focus on solid analysis rather than hype. Make a habit of learning something new each week. Over time, these efforts will compound your knowledge just as your investments compound your wealth.

By taking these steps, you will discover something important: building digital wealth is not about luck or perfect timing. It is about process, patience, and the courage to begin even when you do not have every answer. Think of the examples you read earlier in this book. Real investors started with only a few dollars and many questions, made mistakes but learned from them, and steadily built their portfolios over time.

You can do the same. You're already ahead of the curve because you've equipped yourself with knowledge, skepticism, and a commitment to continuous improvement. Every successful crypto investor was once a beginner, unsure of what to do next. The difference between those who thrive and those who falter is simple: action grounded in education and self-discipline.

The reality is that digital finance is not going away; it's only becoming a larger part of the global economy. The old boundaries between asset classes are dissolving. Crypto is no longer a fringe experiment; it's quickly moving into the mainstream, reshaping how people save, invest, and think about money itself. By stepping in now, thoughtfully and responsibly, you position yourself at the forefront of this transformation.

Remember, wealth without limits isn't built overnight. But it is available to anyone willing to start, stay smart, and keep learning. Don't let fear or perfectionism keep you on the sidelines. Every great investor was once a newcomer, every expert once asked their first question, and every thriving portfolio started with a single trade.

In closing, your journey toward digital wealth begins not with a leap, but with a single step, a decision to take control of your financial future. Start small, stay curious, remain disciplined, and make learning a regular habit. Crypto investing rewards those who prepare, who wait, and who act, not rashly, but with purpose.

Your new wealth starts here, today. What you do in the next 90 days could lay the groundwork for a lifetime of financial freedom. So, as you close this book, remember: you don't need to be a technical expert to win in this space. You just need a plan, a willingness to take action, and the resilience to keep going.

This is your invitation. The tools, the knowledge, and the strategies are now yours. Step forward, and let your path to wealth without limits begin now.

www.ingramcontent.com/pod-product-compliance
Lightning Source LLC
Chambersburg PA
CBHW050529240926
51846CB00003B/753

* 9 7 8 1 9 7 0 8 3 9 1 5 9 *